Model Building in Mathematical Programming

Author
Dr (Er) Om Prakash
Professor SMS Lucknow

Outline

Lecture 1: Modelling and Mathematical Programming

1. The general process of mathematical modelling

Mathematical modelling is a complex process. For the moment, we will consider the following simplistic representation of the modelling process. This will be further refined in the following lectures.

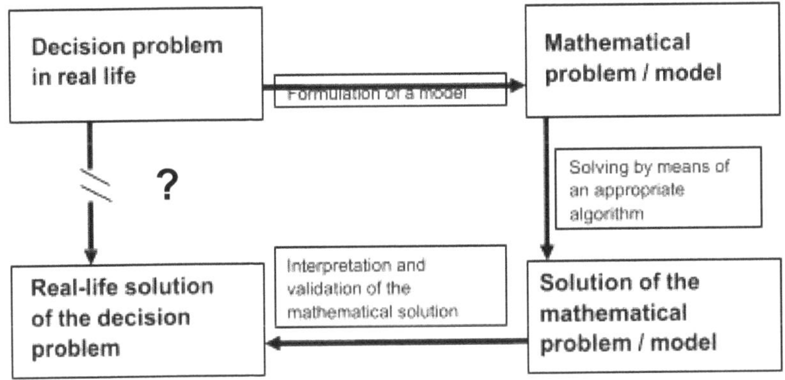

During the process of modelling, it is important that we clearly distinguish between the reality "out there" (reality I) and the mathematical reality of the model (reality II). For providing a successful solution of a real-life decision problem, it is vital to ensure that we create the mathematical reality (the model) in a way that it corresponds to our understanding (i.e. interpretation) of the problem in real life with respect to all aspects that we deem important.

Note that both the process of formulating a model and the process of interpreting its solution are creative acts of re-interpretation. It is not uncommon that, during these processes, modellers enhance their understanding of both the mathematical structure they use (reality II) and the decision problem in real life (reality I).

2. An example of a Mathematical Programming problem

Before we introduce a general definition of what a Mathematical Programming problem is, let us start with an example. This problem is a so-called Linear Programming problem, which can generally be regarded as the most important subtype of a Mathematical Programming problem and is the main type of problem to be addressed in this course.

The Product Mix Model:

Consider problem of Exercise 1 (see page 8). The seven activities of the farmer may be growing of 7 different crops, say crop 1 to crop 7. She has two scarce resources, namely land and labour. The problem is to decide the profit maximizing product mix.

Let us analyse the problem by asking 4 questions:

1. *Who is the decision-maker?* The farmer.
2. *What is the farmer's objective?* To maximise her revenue.
3. *What can the farmer vary/change?* The amounts of each crop to grow.
4. *What restricts the farmer's actions?* The amounts of land and labour.

The answer to the third question provides us with the decision variables of the problem. Let *crops* be the set of possible crops indexed by j. Let x_j be the level at which activity j is to be undertaken, with $j = 1,...,7$. These x_j are the decision variables.

The answer to the fourth question provides us with the resource constraints of the problem. This means that, regarding the two resources land and labour, we have the constraint:

Amount of resource used ≤ Amount available.

The table of data in Problem 1 tells us that one unit level of activity 1 (e.g. growing 100 tons of wheat) requires 19 hectares of land and 10 man-weeks of labour. We will assume that half a unit of activity 1 will then require 9.5 hectares of land and 5 man-weeks of labour, while 100 units will require 1900 hectares and 1000 man-weeks respectively. So we will assume that there are no economies or diseconomies of scale in our model.
What we want is the best production plan within the available resources. If we decide to have all activities at the same level, for example, we can have no more than (just under) three units of each, because 153 man-weeks are required for making three of everything. So we assume that the total use of a resource is just the sum of amounts used for each activity.

On the basis of these assumptions and given the above definition of the decision variables x_j, we can express our resource constraints in the following way:

$$19x_1 + 1x_2 + 1x_3 + 2x_4 + 10x_5 + 5x_6 + 8x_7 \leq 200$$

$$10x_1 + 1x_2 + 6x_3 + 15x_4 + 17x_5 + 1x_6 + 1x_7 \leq 150 .$$

The answer of the second question provides us with the objective function of the model. We will assume that the farmer's revenue is just the sum of the revenues given by the seven activities. Given the above definition of the decision variables x_j, we can express our objective function in the following way:

$$1200x_1 + 80x_2 + 240x_3 + 400x_4 + 1200x_5 + 200x_6 + 240_7 .$$

Obviously our problem has two resource constraints in seven decision variables. Because both the constraints and the objective function are linear in the decision variables, we call our problem a 2x7 Linear Programming problem. In fact, it has seven more constraints, namely $x_j \geq 0$ for all j, i.e. only non-negative levels of all activities are allowed. These constraints are called non-negativities and are typically assumed for a Linear Programming problem.

In sum, our mathematical model reads as follows:

maximise

$$1200x_1 \square\ 80x_2 \square\ 240x_3 \square\ 400x_4 \square 1200x_5 \square\ 200x_6 \square\ 240$$

subject to

$$19x_1 \square 1x_2 \square 1x_3 \square\ 2x_4 \square 10x_5 \square\ 5x_6 \square\ 8x_7 \square\ 200$$

$$10x_1 \square 1x_2 \square\ 6x_3 \square 15x_4 \square 17x_5 \square 1x_6 \square 1x_7 \square\ 150$$

$x_j \square\ 0$, $x_j \square\square$ **for all** j=1,2,....,7.

We can use AMPLDev for solving this mathematical problem. If we translate our mathematical model into the programming language AMPL, it reads as follows (note the American-English spelling):

```
var x1 >= 0;
var x2 >= 0;
var x3 >= 0;
var x4 >= 0;
var x5 >= 0;
var x6 >= 0;
var x7 >= 0;

maximize

revenue:
        1200*x1 + 80*x2 + 240*x3 + 400*x4 + 1200*x5 +200*x6 + 240*x7;

subject to

land:
        19*x1 + x2 + x3 + 2*x4 + 10*x5 + 5*x6 + 8*x7 <= 200; manweeks:
        10*x1 + x2 + 6*x3 + 15*x4 + 17*x5 + x6 + x7 <= 150;
```

Solving this problem using AMPL Studio (the predecessor of AMPLDev) leads to the following output:

```
AmplStudio Modeling System - Copyright (c) 2003-2010, Datumatic Ltd

MODEL.STATISTICS

Problem name        :Lecture1_exercise1
Pathname            :H:\Teaching\2010-11\OR428\Lecture_Notes\OR428
                    :_AMPL_files\OR428_exercises\
Model Filename      :"Lecture1_exercise1.mod"
Data Filename       :"Lecture1_exercise1.dat"
Date                :1:5:2011
Time                :15:53
Constraints         :2          : Nonzeros
S_Constraints       :2
Variables           :7          : Nonzeros

SOLUTION.RESULT

'Optimal solution found'

FortMP 3.2j: LP OPTIMAL SOLUTION, Objective = 14798.206278026906


DECISION.VARIABLES

 Variable  Activity  U bound  ReducedCost

1 x1     8.52018  Infinity 1.13687e-13
5 x5     3.81166  Infinity 0

CONSTRAINTS

   Name        Slack        Body     Dual

1 land       -2.84217e-14   200     37.6682
2 manweeks   0              150     48.4305

END
```

If we interpret these mathematical results (admittedly, in this simple case there is not much to interpret), we get the following solution to our real-life decision problem:

Only two activities need to be considered, crop 1 at level 8.52 and crop 5 at level 3.82. This will lead to the maximal possible revenue of £14,798.21 (the other numbers calculated by AMPL Studio/ AMPLDev will be explained at a later stage in the course).

3. The general form of Mathematical Programming problems

3.1 Linear Programming problems

In general, Linear Programming problems involve determining the *optimal* values of the decision variables , i.e. those which maximise (or minimise) a linear objective function subject to linear constraints and the non-negativities.

In the farmer's problem the decision variables are the amounts of crops to be grown, and the resource constraints are the constraints on the land and labour. The non-negativities are the constraints that ensure that a non-negative amount of crops is grown. The objective function is to maximise profit. We can put this in a more general form and define a General Linear Programming (LP) problem as follows:

Definition of General Linear Programming problems

maximise (or minimise) $c_1x_1 \square c_2x_2 \square \ldots \square c_nx_n$

subject to $a_{11}x_1 \square a_{12}x_2 \square \ldots \square a_{1n}x_n \square\square b_1$

$a_{21}x_1 \square a_{22}x_2 \square \ldots \square a_{2n}x_n \square\square b_2$

$\vdots$

$a_{m1}x_1 \square a_{m2}x_2 \square \ldots \square a_{mn}x_n \square\square b_m$

$x_j \square 0, j \square 1,2,\ldots, n$

In this definition, the number of decision variables is n, the number of resource constraints is m, and <> mean a mixture of $\leq$, $\geq$, and = constraints. Moreover, there are n non-negativity constraints.

It is often convenient to refer to a standardised version of the LP problem defined above. To derive one for our purposes we will use a number of very simple observations. First, we may convert a minimisation LP problem to a maximisation LP problem by negating the objective function (minimising $\sum_j c_jx_j$ is equivalent to maximising $-\sum_j c_jx_j$). Similarly, we may rewrite any constraint of the form $\sum_j a_{ij}x_j \geq b_i$ as $-(\sum_j a_{ij}x_j) \leq -b_i$. Finally, we may replace an equality constraint $\sum_j a_{ij}x_j = b_i$ by the two inequalities $\sum_j a_{ij}x_j \leq b_i$, $\sum_j a_{ij}x_j \geq b_i$ (and then rewrite the second one as $-(\sum_j a_{ij}x_j) \leq -b_i$). By applying these rules to any LP problem we may restate it in a **maximisation standard form** or a **minimisation standard form**. These are given below in matrix notation, where If c and $\tilde{c}$ are an n-dimensional vectors of the coefficients of the objective function, x *is* an n-dimensional vector of the variables, A and $\tilde{A}$ are mxn-matrices of the resource constraints (with the 'technological coefficients' a_{ij}), b and $\tilde{b}$ are m-dimensional vectors of the coefficients of the 'right hand sides' (RHS) of the resource constraints, 0 is an n-dimensional vector of zeros and I denotes the identity matrix (so that $\tilde{c} = -c$, $\tilde{b} = -b$ and $\tilde{A} = -A$):

Definition of Linear Programming Problems in standard forms

(a) maximise cx (b) minimise $\tilde{c}x$

subject to $Ax \leq b$

subject to

$$Ax \geq b$$

$$Ix \geq 0$$

$$Ix \geq 0$$

We can distinguish between two sub-types of LP problems: if we are only interested in a solution that fulfils the constraints $Ax \leq b$ and $x \geq 0$, we can speak of a *feasibility* problem; if we would like to find a solution that both fulfils the constraints $Ax \leq b$ and $x \geq 0$ and maximises the objective function cx, we have an *optimisation* problem.
As we have also seen in the above example, modelling a problem as an LP problem involves (at least) three assumptions:

1. The decision variables are independent.
2. The resources are homogeneous and infinitely divisible (-> resource constraints).
3. There are no economies and diseconomies of scale (-> objective function).

LP problems are the most prominent examples of Mathematical Programming problems. The first mathematical LP problems were investigated by Fourier, among others, over a hundred years ago. However, applied LP in the modern sense began in the 1940's with Dantzig in the USA and Kantorovich in the former USSR and turned out to be a successful tool for planning military operations in WWII.

This is also the historical origin of the term "programming" in "Linear Programming", "Integer Programming", "Mathematical Programming", etc. In these days, the military referred to the process of planning their operations as "programming". So "Linear Programming" should not be confused with programming in the sense of "programming computers"; in fact, "Linear Programming" as such, as a type of mathematical problem and as a subfield of Operational Research, has nothing to do with computer programming. Because Linear Programming problems are normally tackled by means of computers when it comes to solving larger real-life problems, this confusion is perhaps inevitable. However, for the process of modelling, it is important to clearly distinguish between mathematical "Linear Programming" problems and the tools (computers and a programming language such as AMPL, for example) by means of which these mathematical problems are solved.

The basic LP model is very simple mathematically, but very versatile. It has been applied in engineering, production planning, marketing, distribution, finance, etc., etc. Modern applications include a model for comparing the efficiency of branches of an organisation and aiding pathologists in diagnosing breast cancer (see also the table of Linear Programming applications at the end of these lecture notes). Models with thousands of variables and constraints frequently arise in practical problems and are being solved routinely, and even LP models with more than a million variables and constraints often do not pose significant problems nowadays (see table at the end of these lecture notes).

3.2 General Mathematical Programming problems

Our definition of an LP problem can be generalised to a larger class of mathematical problems in order to allow for feasibility and optimisation problems with arbitrary (i.e. non-linear) objective functions and arbitrary resource constraints. This leads to the following definition where x is an n-vector (the *decision variables*), $f : X \subseteq R^n \rightarrow R$ a function (the *objective function*) with a domain that is a subset X of the n- dimensional real space and maps into the real space, and $g : X \subseteq R^n \rightarrow R^m$ a function (the *resource constraints*) that maps from X into the m-dimensional real space:

Definition Mathematical Programming problem

$$\begin{aligned} \text{maximise} \quad & f(x) \\ \text{subject to} \quad & g(x) \leq 0, \\ & x \in X \end{aligned}$$

If we just aim at finding an $x \in X$ that satisfies the inequality $\mathbf{g(x)} \leq \mathbf{0}$, we speak of a *feasibility* problem; if we look for an $x \in X$ that both satisfies the inequality $\mathbf{g(x)} \leq \mathbf{0}$ and maximises the function $\mathbf{f(x)}$, we have an *optimisation* problem. Note that in practical applications it is sometimes sufficient to find an $x \in X$ such that $\mathbf{f(x)}$ is near-optimal. This would be an optimisation problem where we look for an *approximation* of the optimal solution.

3.3 Other special types of Mathematical Programming problems

Based on the general definition of a Mathematical Programming problem, operational researchers and mathematicians have studied many special types of Mathematical Programming problems, examined their properties and suggested specific algorithms for solving them. Among these are, for example, Convex Programming problems (where the objective function is concave, and the resource constraints and the condition $x \in X$ define a convex set), and Separable Programming problems (where the functions $\mathbf{f(x)}$ and $\mathbf{g(x)}$ can be written as sums of functions each summand of which depends only on one component of the n-vector x). The Mathematical Programming Glossary at

http://glossary.computing.society.informs.org/index.php?page=nature.html

provides an excellent overview about many different types of Mathematical Programming problems.

Another type of Mathematical Programming problems covered in this course are **Integer Programming** problems, where:

$$\mathbf{f(x)} = c_1 x_1 + c_2 x_2 + \ldots + c_n x_n \text{ and } \mathbf{g(x)} = \mathbf{Ax} - \mathbf{b},$$

as in the Linear Programming problem, and $x \in Z^n$, i.e. x must be an integer vector. If only some of the components of x are required to be integer, and both the objective function and the resource constraints are linear, we speak of a *Mixed Integer Programming* problem.

Apart from discussing Linear Programming and Integer Programming, the course will also show ways in which some other types of Mathematical Programming problems can fruitfully be solved to optimality or near-optimality by representing it as a Linear Programming problem.

4. Reading and exercises

Exercises and tasks:

1. Programme and solve the Product Mix Problem of the lecture (Exercise 1) with AMPLDev. The chapter 4- 6 of the AMPLDev User Manual (pages 15-34, uploaded on Moolde) will help you with making your first steps with AMPLDev. Attend the Computer Help Session in week 3 if you encounter any problems with this.

2. Solve problems 3 and 4 by formulating a mathematical model and solving it with AMPLDev.

3. Given the data of exercise 2, find out by means of a Mathematical Programming model and AMPLDev how many units of products X and Y the company should produce to maximize profit. Can you find *two different* ways of modelling the problem (which lead to the same solution, of course)?

4. Answer question (a) in exercise 6 by setting up a mathematical model and solving it with AMPLDev. Have you got an idea of how to address question (b)?

5. Download the full AMPLDev User Manual.

Reading

Required:

The chapter 4-6 of the AMPLDev User Manual which can has been uploaded on the course's Moodle page.

Recommended:

Chapter 1 (pages 1-9) of Williams, H.P. (1999).

Suggested:

a) Chapters 1 and/or 2 (pages 1-23) of Hillier, F.S. and Liebermann, G.J. (2001);

b) "The Nature of Mathematical Programming" by George B. Dantzig, one of the 'fathers' of Mathematical Programming, which you can find on http://glossary.computing.society.informs.org/index.php?page=nature.html.

Exercise 1

A 'farmer' has listed seven possible activities in which he might engage as follows:

1	2	3	4	5	6	7	
19 10	1 1	1 6	2 15	10 17	5 1	8 1	hectares of land needed p.a. manweeks labour p.a.
1200	80	240	400	1200	200	240	£ per annum net revenue

The farmer has 200 hectares of land, and his own and his family's labour amounts to 150 manweeks per annum. Which activities should the farmer engage in?

Exercise 2

A firm has two processes, each of which jointly produces products X and Y.

	Process I	Process II
Labour manhours per thousand X Machine hours per thousand X Kilowatt hours per thousand X Output of Y per thousand X	10 3 25 500	15 2 18 750

There is an upper limit on the availability of labour per week of 150 manhours, and 30 hours of machine capacity. There is no restriction on the availability of electricity or on the sales of X and Y; wages and prices are as follows:

Wages per manhour £.75 Price of electricity per kwh £.01 Selling price of X per 1000 £6.00 Selling price of Y per 1000 £9.00

Exercise 3

A firm of shoemakers can produce shoes for men, women and children. The output of women's shoes must be not less than 50% of the total. Each kind of shoe requires a certain type of machine and some skilled labour, and the number of machines and skilled workers available is fixed.

	Men's shoes	Women's shoes	Children's shoes
Machine time required (hours per pair)	1.5	2	1
Skilled labour time required (hours per pair)	2.5	6	1.5
Net profit (pence per pair)	130	280	70

The firm has 20 machines and the labour to man them, and a staff of 50 skilled men. Normal working is 40 hours per week. What rate of production per week maximizes net profit?

Exercise 4

A smallholder owns six hectares of land, and wishes to decide how much to plant with flowers and how much with strawberries. Only one crop can be grown on a particular piece of land in a year. He calculates the average return (that is, proceeds of sale less costs of bulbs/plants and fertilisers, etc.) to be
£800 per hectare for flowers and £1000 per hectare for strawberries. However, the time he has for cultivation and picking is somewhat limited, and the labour requirements by season are as follows (in man-hours per hectare):

	Winter	Spring	Summer	Autumn
Flowers	10	40	0	10
Strawberries	10	20	50	10

The total labour available in hours varies with season: winter, 100 hours; spring, 200 hours; summer, 200 hours; and autumn, 100 hours.

(a) What pattern of crops would you recommend the smallholder to grow?

(b) How much would you recommend that he should be willing to pay for extra labour during each season?

Exercise 5

An airline company is considering the purchase of new long-range, medium-range, and short-range jet passenger aeroplanes. The purchase price would be £6,700,000 for each long-range plane, £5,000,000 for each medium-range plane, and £3,500,000 for each short-range plane. The Board of Directors has authorized a maximum commitment of £150,000,000 for these purchases. Regardless of which aeroplanes are purchased, air travel of all distances is expected to be sufficiently large that these planes would be utilized at essentially maximum capacity. It is estimated that the net annual profit (after subtracting capital recovery costs) would be £420,000 per long-range plane, £300,000 per medium- range plane, and £230,000 per short-range plane.

It is predicted that enough trained pilots will be available to the company to man 30 new aeroplanes. If only short-range planes were purchased, the maintenance facilities would be able to handle 40 new planes. However, each medium-range plane is equivalent to one and one-third short-range planes, and each long-range plane is equivalent to one and two-thirds short-range planes in terms of their use of the maintenance facilities.

The information given above was obtained by a preliminary analysis of the problem. A more detailed analysis will be conducted subsequently. However, using the above data as a first approximation, management wishes to know how many planes of each type should be purchased in order to maximize profit. (You may ignore the fact that the number of airplanes must be an integer).

Some Application Areas of Mathematical Programming

Industry	Applications
Petroleum	Refinery Optimisation, Distribution, Blending, Resource Allocation,
Chemicals	Blending, Resource Allocation
Manufacturing	Product Mix, Resource Allocation, Blending
Transport	Distribution, Depot Location, Scheduling
Finance	Portfolio Selection, Taxation
Agriculture	Crop Rotation, Feed Mix Blending, Distribution
Health	Resource Allocation, Scheduling
Mining	Resource Allocation, Blending
Manpower Planning	Recruitment, Redundancy, Retraining Allocations
Food	Blending, Distribution
Pulp and Paper	Resource Allocation, Minimising Waste, Recycling
Advertising	Media Scheduling
Defence	Resource Allocation, Military Installation Siting
Economic Planning	Extended Input-Output Models

OR 428 – Model Building in Mathematical Programming

Lecture 2: Feasibility I

Outline:

1. **Feasible region**
2. **Is a point feasible?**
3. **Basic and extreme points**
4. **The feasible region in higher dimensions**
5. **Reading and exercises**

1. Feasible region

We will consider only the constraints of a problem, ignoring the objective function until the next chapter. Here we consider an example with only 2 variables as it can easily be represented by a diagram. Consider the feasible region defined by the following set of constraints:

$$2x_1 + x_2 \leq 10$$

$$x_1 + 2x_2 \leq 10$$

$$x_1 + x_2 \leq 6\ x_1$$

$$+\ 3x_2 \leq 12$$

$$3x_1 - x_2 \geq 0\ x_1$$

$$+\ 4x_2 \geq 4\ x_1 \geq$$

$$0,\ x_2 \geq 0.$$

We can represent each constraint in (x_1, x_2) space. The non-negativities imply that only the positive quadrant including the axes needs to be considered. The hatchings indicate the forbidden - infeasible - side of the constraints. A constraint $2x_1 + x_2 \leq 10$ can be represented by the defining equality $2x_1 + x_2 = 10$ with hatching to indicate the disallowed side as in Figure 1 below:

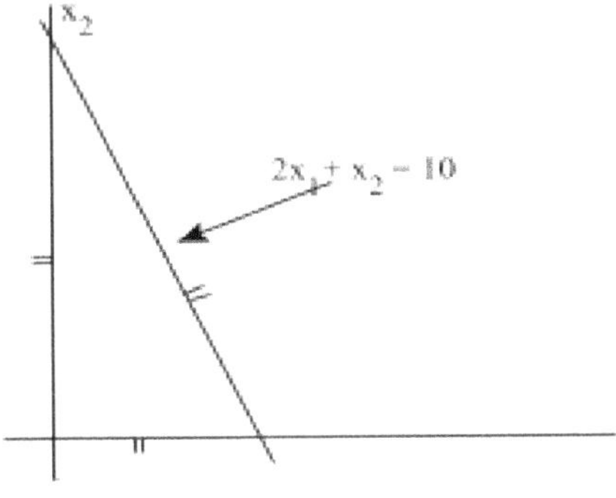

Figure 1

The 6 constraints (including the non-negativities) restrict the allowed values of x_1 and x_2 to the *feasible region* lying on the feasible side of each constraint. That is the area bounded by the points ABCDEF in Figure 2 below:

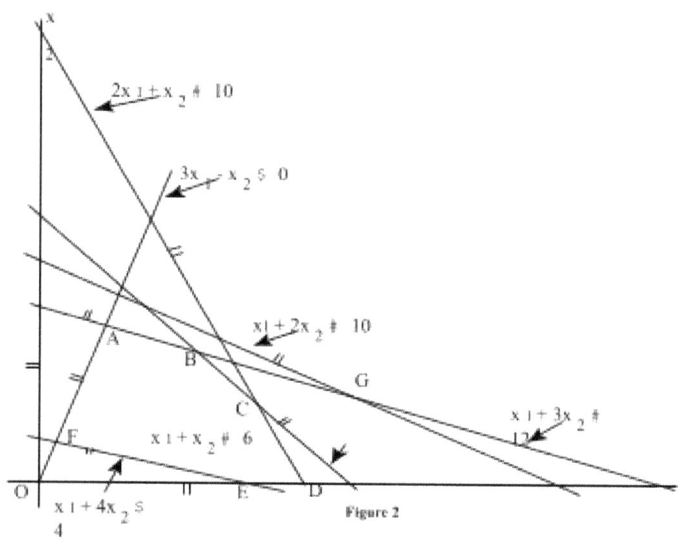

Figure 2

x_1

2. Is a point feasible?

To test whether a point is feasible it is necessary to check that it satisfies all the constraints. For example is the point $x_1 = 1$, $x_2 = 2$ feasible? Substitute the values of x_1 and x_2 into all the constraints:

2*1 + 1*2 = 4 < 10 ✓
1*1 + 2*2 = 5 < 10 ✓
1*1 + 1*2 = 3 < 6 ✓
1*1 + 3*2 = 7 < 12 ✓
3*1 - 1*2 = 1 > 0 ✓
1*1 + 4*2 = 9 > 4 ✓
1 > 0, 2 > 0 ✓✓

The point is feasible as it satisfies all the constraints. In terms of the figure the point (1, 2) lies within the feasible region, ABCDEF.

Consider the constraints:

$$Ax \leq b, x \geq 0.$$

Is a point x^* feasible? Substitute the values x^* into each constraint and check whether the result is $\leq$ the right hand side, that is the element of b. The point x^* is feasible if

$$Ax^* \text{ is } \leq b \text{ and } x^* \text{ is } \geq 0,$$

otherwise the point x^* is infeasible.

3. Basic and Extreme points

Definition

In 2-dimensional space, that is (x_1, x_2) space, a basic point is defined as the point at the intersection of 2 independent equalities (that define constraints of the feasible region). In Figure 2 the basic point labelled B is defined by the intersection of:

$$x_1 + x_2 = 6, \text{ and}$$
$$x_1 + 3x_2 = 12.$$

Basic point D is defined by $2x_1 + x_2 = 10$ and $x_2 = 0$. Basic points B and D are feasible. Basic point G, defined by $x_1 + 2x_2 = 10$ and $x_1 + 3x_2 = 12$, is infeasible.

In n-dimensional space (n variables), a **basic point** is defined as the point at the intersection of n independent equalities (that define constraints of the feasible region). That is a basic point, x^*, is defined by the n independent equalities:

$$Rx^* = b^R,$$

where R is a nxn square matrix and b^R contains the RHS coefficients of the n constraints that define x^*.

In n-dimensional space, if the point x^* is **both basic and feasible**, then it is an **extreme point** of the feasible region. In Figure 2, Points B and D are extreme points while point G is not.

Checking if a point is basic.

In 2-dimensional space, to determine whether a point is basic it is necessary to substitute the values of x_1 and x_2 into the constraints and determine whether 2 (or more) of them are satisfied as equalities. Consider the point $x_1 = 4$, $x_2 = 2$, (point C in Figure 2): substituting the values into the all the constraints shows that it is basic as constraints 1 and constraint 3 are satisfied as equalities. Point C is an extreme point as these calculations show that it is feasible as well as basic.

In n-dimensional space to determine whether point, x^*, is basic:

1. compute Ax^* and compare it with b, and compare x^* with 0;
2. determine whether n or independent constraints are satisfied as equalities, if (and only if) this is the case then x^* is basic, otherwise x^* is not basic.

The n satisfied constraints may be all resource constraints, or all non-negativities, or a mixture of resource constraints and non-negativities.

Checking if a basic point is an extreme point.

In Figure 2 the basic point A is defined by the independent constraints:

$$x_1 + 3x_2 = 12 \text{ and}$$
$$3x_1 - x_2 = 0.$$

Solving these two simultaneous equations gives $x_1 = 1.2$ and $x_2 = 3.6$. Substituting the values of x_1 and x_2 into all the constraints shows that it is a feasible point and hence an extreme point.

In n-dimensions, Consider that a basic point is defined by the n independent equations (which define constraints of the feasible region):

$$Rx = b^R.$$

Solve these n equations to give x^*. Then substitute x^* into the constraints and compute Ax^*. If and only if $Ax^* \leq b$ and $x^* \geq 0$ then x^* is feasible and so $x^*$is an extreme point of the feasible region.

A note on Degeneracy

Note that there may be more than n constraints that are satisfied as equalities at a basic point. In such a case there may be more than one way to choose a subset of n linearly independent constraints to *define* that point. Basic points which do not have a unique definition are called *degenerate*. Degeneracy complicates the verification of optimality for LP. We shall consider this in subsequent lectures.

Consider the example in Figure 3 below. Points A, B, C, D are basic points: each lies on the intersection of two linearly independent equalities that correspond to constraints of the feasible region. Note that B is a degenerate basic point because it lies on the intersection of three equalities, any pair of which are linearly independent. Basic points A,B,C are also feasible and so they are extreme points of the feasible region. Hence, point B is a degenerate extreme point.

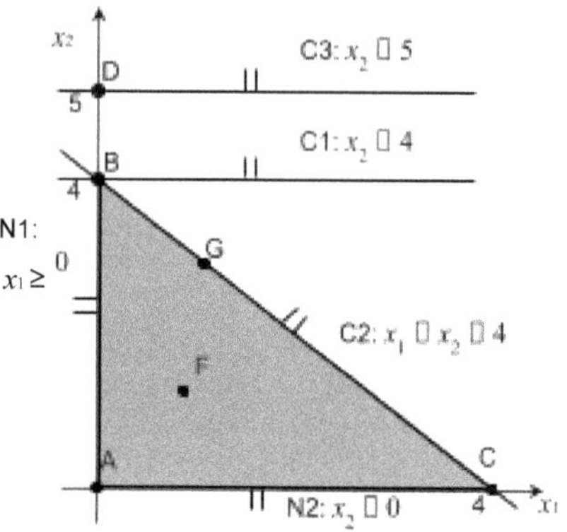

Figure 3

4. The feasible region in higher dimensions

In higher dimensions (i.e. n variables x_j) the boundaries of the feasible region are given by <u>hyperplanes</u> ('planes' in 3 dimensions)

$$\{(x_1, x_2, ..., x_n) \in R^n : a_{i1} x_1 + a_{i2} x_2 + ... + a_{in} x_n = b_i\}$$

or, in vector notation,

$$\{x \in R^n : a_i . x = b_i\}.$$

These hyperplanes define <u>affine half-spaces</u>

$$\{x \in R^n : a_i . x \leq b_i\} \text{ (for } a_i . \neq 0 \text{).}$$

The intersection of these half-spaces is the feasible region, which is a <u>(convex) polyhedron</u>

$$\{x \in R^n : Ax \leq b\},$$

which might be <u>bounded.</u> (A bounded polyhedron is called a <u>polytope.</u>)

(A set of points S is called <u>convex</u> if for any pair of points (x, y) in S all points on the line that connects

x with y are also elements of S.)

The basic points and the extreme points of the feasible region lie at the intersection of n independent hyperplanes.

5. Reading and exercises

Exercise 1

Consider the constraints

$$3x_1 + 2x_2 \geq 60$$

$$-x_1 + 2x_2 \leq 20$$

$$x_1 \leq 30$$

$$x_1 - x_2 \leq 30$$

$$x_1, x_2 \geq 0$$

(a) Identify the extreme points of the feasible region. (Determine algebraically the values of the variables and show algebraically that the points are feasible.)

(b) Identify an infeasible basic point. (Determine algebraically the values of the variables and show algebraically that the point is infeasible.)

Reading

Recommended: chapter 3 of Hillier, F.S and Liebermann, G.J. (2001)

Suggested: chapters 2.1 to 2.5 of Bertsimas, D. and Tsitsiklis, J.N. (1997)

OR 428 – Model Building in Mathematical Programming

Lecture 3: Linear Programming II - Feasibility II and Optimality I

Outline:

1. **Feasibility II – Derived constraints**
2. **Optimality I – The objective function as contours**
3. **Optimality I – Properties of the optimal contour**
4. **Optimality I – Optimality conditions**
5. **Reading and exercises**

1. Feasibility II - Derived constraints

In Lecture 2 we have examined the shape of the feasible region and seen that it is a convex set bounded by lines (in 2 dimensions, i.e. with 2 decision variables), planes (in 3 dimensions), or hyperplanes (in n dimensions). We will now address another property of the feasible region as a prerequisite for analysing optimality.
Our question is: how can we derive new constraints from the resource constraints given by $\mathbf{Ax} \leq \mathbf{b}$ such that that all points that satisfy $\mathbf{Ax} \leq \mathbf{b}$ also satisfy the new constraint (i.e. the feasible set will remain the same if we add these new constraints) **and** some extreme point satisfies this new constraint as an equality (i.e. the new constraint 'touches' an extreme point)?

Combining uniform inequalities
One can add together positive and negative multiples of equalities and derive a new equality that is satisfied by the same values that satisfy the original equalities. It is not possible to do exactly the same with inequalities. If we have a uniform set of linear inequalities, that is all expressed as $\leq$ then we can add together non-negative multiples of them to derive a new valid $\leq$ linear inequality (and the same holds for $\geq$ inequalities). The newly formed inequality is valid in the sense that all points that are feasible with respect to the original inequalities is feasible with respect to the new in equality.

Combining 2 uniform inequalities in 2 dimensions
In 2-dimensional space taking a non-negative weighted combination of 2 uniform inequalities derives a new valid inequality which is satisfied as an equality at the point of intersection of the 2 original inequalities. For example consider the following two constraints:

$$2x_1 + x_2 \leq 10$$
$$x_1 + 3x_2 \leq 12,$$

which intersect at $x_1 = 3.6$, $x_2 = 2.8$. Deriving a new constraint with arbitrarily chosen weights of 2 and 1 gives

$$\begin{aligned} &2*(2x_1 + x_2 \leq 10) \\ +\ &1*(x_1 + 3x_2 \leq 12) \\ =\ &5x_1 + 5x_2 \leq 32. \end{aligned}$$

The point $x_1 = 3.6$, $x_2 = 2.8$ satisfies $5x_1 + 5x_2 \leq 32$ as an equality. This relationship is illustrated in Figure 1 below.

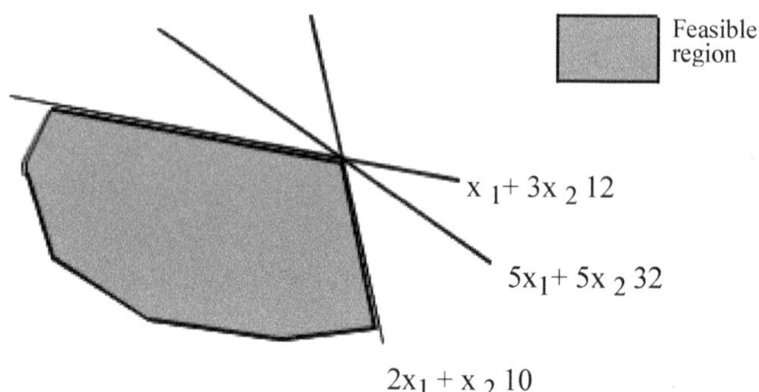

Figure 1

Combining n uniform inequalities in n dimensions

Similarly, in n-dimensional space, taking a non-negative weighted combination of $n \leq$ linear inequalities derives a new $\leq$ inequality which is satisfied as an equality at the point of intersection of the n original inequalities. Let R, be an nxn square matrix, and consider the feasible defined by (assume this is non-empty):

$$Rx \leq g.$$

The point of intersection is x^*, that is $Rx^* = g.$

Let w be an n-vector of non-negative values, that is $w \geq 0$, then we may derive a new inequality as follows:

$$wRx \leq wg.$$

Define $d = wR$, and $\gamma = wg$ so that the above may be rewritten in the new valid inequality:

$$dx \leq \gamma.$$

The point of intersection, x^*, also satisfies the new constraint as an equality, i.e.:

$$dx^* = \gamma.$$

Using 0 weights in a combination

In 2 dimensional space, with more than 2 linear inequalities all expressed as $\leq$ inequalities, if we use non-negative weights for 2 inequalities and a weight of 0 for the others we will derive a new valid inequality. The new inequality is satisfied as an equality at the intersection of the 2 inequalities with non-negative weights. A valid inequality means that all points satisfying the 2 original inequalities, with non-negative weights, also satisfy the new inequality.

For example, consider expressing the example in Lecture 2 as a uniform set of $\leq$ constraints. The resource constraints are multiplied by -1 if necessary to convert an $\geq$ inequality to a $\leq$ inequality and the non-negativities are also multiplied by -1:

$$2x_1 + x_2 \leq 10$$
$$1x_1 + 2x_2 \leq 10$$
$$x_1 + x_2 \leq 6$$
$$x_1 + 3x_2 \leq 12$$
$$-3x_1 + x_2 \leq 0$$
$$-x_1 - 4x_2 \leq -4$$
$$-1x_1 + 0x_2 \leq 0$$
$$0x_1 - 1x_2 \leq 0.$$

Taking weights (arbitrarily chosen) of 1 on constraint 1, 3 on constraint 3, and 0 on all the others derives a new valid inequality:

$$
\begin{aligned}
&1*(2x_1 + x_2 \leq 10)\\
&+ 0*(1x_1 + 2x_2 \leq 10)\\
&+ 3*(x_1 + x_2 \leq 6)\\
&+ 0*(x_1 + 3x_2 \leq 12)\\
&+ 0*(-3x_1 + x_2 \leq 0)\\
&+0*(-x_1 - 4x_2 \leq -4)\\
&+0*(-1x_1 + 0x_2 \leq 0)\\
&+0*(0x_1 - 1x_2 \leq 0)\\
&= 5x_1 + 4x_2 \leq 28.
\end{aligned}
$$

This is illustrated in Figure 2 below:

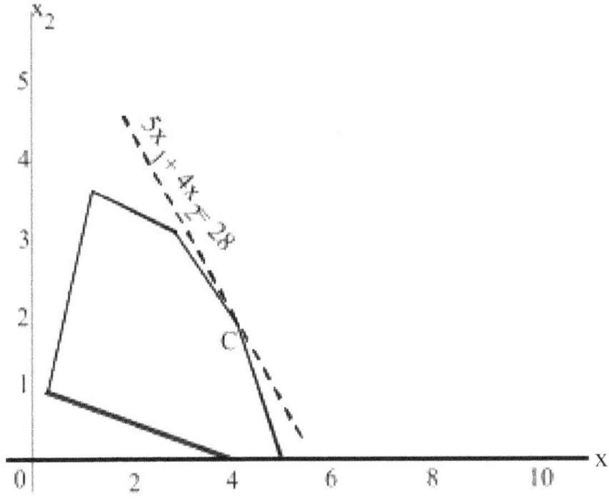

Figure 2

General Statement

In n-dimensional space, with more than n linear inequalities all expressed as $\leq$ inequalities, if we take a combination using non-negative weights for n inequalities and a weight of 0 for the others, we will derive a new valid inequality. The new inequality is satisfied as an equality at the intersection of the n inequalities with non-negative weights. A valid inequality means that all points satisfying the original inequalities also satisfy the new inequality.

Consider the region defined by the following system of constraints:

$$Ax \leq b$$
$$x \geq 0,$$

where x is an n-vector, A is a mxn matrix, and b is a m-vector. Express all the constraints as $\leq$ inequalities:

$$Ax \leq b$$
$$\text{-I}x \leq 0.$$

Take a vector $(y\ w)$ where y is an m-vector and w a n-vector such that exactly m elements (out of the $m+n$) of the vector $(y\ w)$ are $=0$ and the remaining n can be ≥ 0. Multiply the weights by the constraints:

$$[y\ w]\begin{bmatrix} A \\ -I \end{bmatrix} x \leq [y\ w]\begin{bmatrix} b \\ 0 \end{bmatrix}$$

$$\Leftrightarrow (yA - w)x \leq yb$$

$$\Leftrightarrow dx \leq \gamma ,$$

where $d = yA - w$ and $= yb$, to derive a new valid inequality $dx \leq \gamma$,.

Let the n constraints whose weights are ≥ 0 be:

$$Rx \leq g,$$

which intersect at x^*, that is $Rx^* = g$. The new derived constraint also goes through x^*, that is $dx^* = \gamma$.

2. Optimality I – The objective function as contours

Representing the objective function as contours

In 2 dimensions it is possible to represent the objective function by its contour lines. Consider that the objective function to be *maximised* is $2x_1 + 8x_2$. In Figure 3 below, the following set of contour lines for this objective is drawn is drawn:

$$2x_1 + 8x_2 = 8$$
$$2x_1 + 8x_2 = 16$$
$$2x_1 + 8x_2 = 24$$
$$2x_1 + 8x_2 = 32.$$

There are an infinite number of contour lines that could be drawn. In the figure the arrow indicates the direction of increase of the objective function, that is the direction of increasing contours.

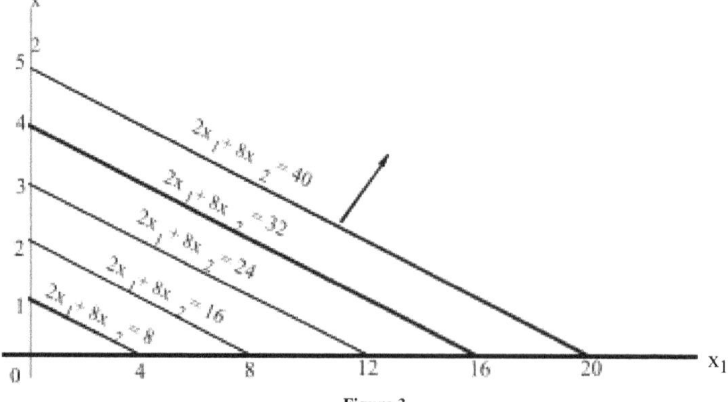

Figure 3

The feasible region and the objective function
In Figure 4, below, the contours of the feasible region are superimposed onto the feasible region, that is Figure 3 is superimposed on Figure 2.

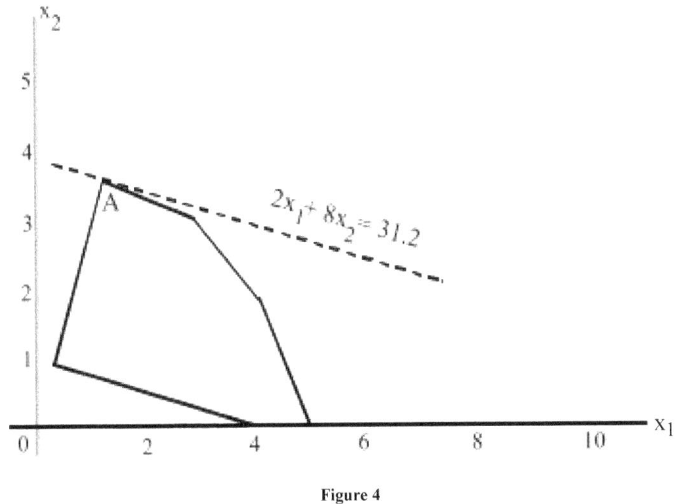

Figure 4

3. Optimality I – Properties of the optimal contour

This example in Figure 4 illustrates two very important characteristics of the optimal contour:

1. A linear function maximised (or minimised) over a feasible region defined by linear constraints achieves its maximum or minimum at an extreme point of the feasible region (although the maximum/minimum may not be unique).

2. All the feasible region lies on one side of the optimal contour, i.e. the optimal contour defines a valid inequality for the feasible region.

The first property means that to determine the optimal point we may restrict our attention to extreme points; we know in advance that (at least) one of them will be optimal. The second property is illustrated in Figure 4. All the feasible region lies within the area defined by: $2x_1 + 8x_2 \leq 31.2$, that is, in the area on the less-than-or-equal-to the optimal (maximum) contour.

In general, if the linear function $cx = c_1x_1 + c_2x_2 + \quad + c_nx_n$, is maximised at an extreme point x^* of the feasible region, attaining the value $\gamma^* = cx^*$, then all the feasible region lies within the area defined by $c_1x_1 + c_2x_2 + \quad + c_nx_n \leq \gamma^*$. Similarly, if the same linear function is minimised at an extreme point x' of the feasible region, attaining the value $\gamma' = cx'$ then all the feasible region lies within the area defined by $c_1x_1 + c_2x_2 + \quad + c_nx_n \geq \gamma'$.

Note that when maximising the feasible region is on the ≤ side of the optimal contour and when minimising the feasible region is on the ≥ side of the optimum contour.

We need to be able to distinguish between the two circumstances below. In both figures the objective function is shown by the - - - - line and the direction of optimisation by the arrow. The constraints are shown with solid lines. In Figure 5 the objective function **is** maximised at the point *. In Figure 6 the objective function **is not** maximised at the point *.

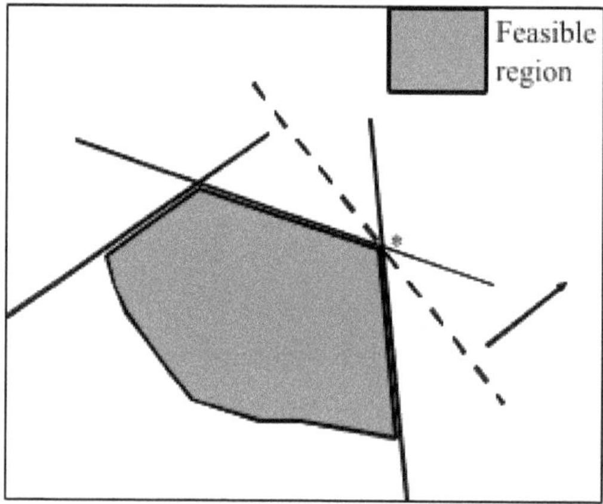

Figure 5

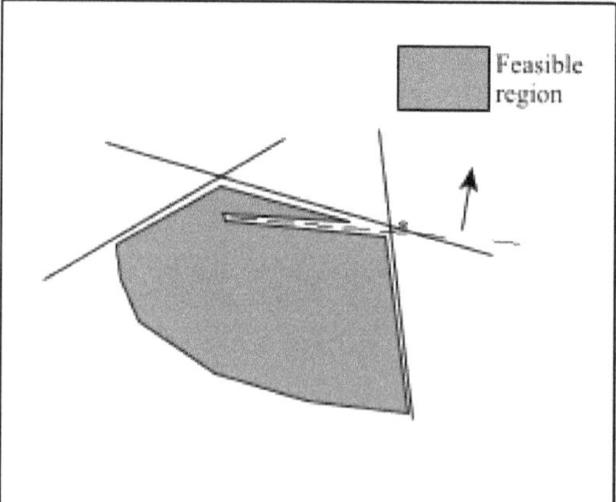

Figure 6

4. Optimality I – Optimality conditions

We have seen that:

(a) we can derive all valid inequalities that satisfy a certain extreme point as an equality by multiplying, with non-negative weights, the *n* resource constraints that define this extreme point and adding them, and

(b) the objective function reaches its maximum (or minimum) at an extreme point of the feasible region with the feasible region being on one side of the optimal contour (i.e. the optimal contour is a valid inequality that satisfies some extreme point as an equality).

These two insights are the ingredients for a test to determine whether or whether not a certain extreme point is optimal: **is it possible to derive a contour of the objective function by calculating a non-negative combination of the constraints defining the extreme point?**

If the answer is yes, then, because of (a), the contour calculated is a valid inequality that satisfies the extreme point as an equality, and therefore, because of (b), this contour must be the optimal contour. Hence the extreme point in question is an optimal solution of our Linear Programming problem. If the answer is no, then, because of (a), there exists no contour of the objective function that is a valid inequality satisfying this extreme point as an equality, and as a consequence, because of (b), the extreme point in question cannot be optimal.

Example

We illustrate the idea using the following example with all the constraints expressed as $\leq$ constraints:

Maximise $2x_1 + 8x_2$ subject

to $2x_1 + x_2 \leq 10$

$1x_1 + 2x_2 \leq 10$

$x_1 + x_2 \leq 6$

$x_1 + 3x_2 \leq 12$

$-3x_1 + x_2 \leq 0$

$-x_1 - 4x_2 \leq -4$

$-1x_1 + 0x_2 \leq 0$

$0x_1 - 1x_2 \leq 0.$

Feasibility

From Figure 4 (and also Figure 2 in Lecture 2) it appears that the optimum is point A. The values of x_1 and x_2 are found by solving constraints 4 and 5 as equalities:

$$x_1 + 3x_2 = 12$$
$$-3x_1 + x_2 = 0,$$

giving $x_1 = 1.2$ and $x_2 = 3.6$. Check that this basic point is feasible:

$$2*1.2 + 1*3.6 = 6 < 10$$
$$1*1.2 + 2*3.6 = 8.4 < 10$$
$$1*1.2 + 1*3.6 = 4.8 < 6$$
$$1*1.2 + 3*3.6 = 12 = 12$$
$$-3*1.2 + 1*3.6 = 0 = 0$$
$$-1*1.2 - 4*3.6 = -15.6 < -4$$
$$-1*1.2 + 0*3.6 = -1.2 < 0$$
$$0*1.2 - 1*3.6 = -3.6 < 0.$$

The point is feasible, so it is an extreme point and hence a candidate for the optimum.

Optimality

Can we find non-negative weights with which to combine constraints 4 and 5, which define point A, in order to derive the objective as a valid inequality? We require:

$$y_4 * (x_1 + 3x_2 \leq 12)$$
$$+ y_5 * (-3x_1 + x_2 \leq 0)$$
$$= 2x_1 + 8x_2 \leq \gamma,$$

where $2x_1 + 8x_2$ is the objective function. We must solve the equations:

$$y_4 - 3y_5 = 2$$
$$3y_4 + y_5 = 8,$$

giving $y_4 = 2.6$, $y_5 = 0.2$ and $\gamma = 31.2$. Notice that we formed these y equations by reading down the columns. Since these weights are both positive we have succeeded in finding weights which enable us to represent the objective function as a derived constraint. So every point that is feasible with respect to the 2 constraints (and so every feasible point):

$$x_1 + 3x_2 \leq 12$$
$$-3x_1 + x_2 \leq 0,$$

must satisfy $2x_1 + 8x_2 \leq 31.2$. The point A, (1.2, 3.6), satisfies this as an equality:

$$2 * 1.2 + 8 * 3.6 = 31.2.$$

It follows that the function is maximised over the feasible region at the point $x_1 = 1.2$, $x_2 = 3.6$ and the value of the objective function is 31.2.

Example

Point C in Figure 2 of lecture 2 is the intersection of constraints 1 and 3:

$$2x_1 + x_2 = 10$$
$$x_1 + x_2 = 6,$$

which when solved give $x_1 = 4$ and $x_2 = 2$. It can be shown, but will not be here, that this basic point is feasible and hence point C is an extreme point and a candidate for the optimum. Is the function $2x_1 + 8x_2$ maximised at C? The equations in the y variables are

$$2y_1 + y_3 = 2$$
$$y_1 + y_3 = 8,$$

which when solved give $y_1 = -6$ and $y_3 = 14$. The negative value for y_1 shows that it is not possible to represent the objective function as a valid constraint. Hence the function $2x_1 + 8x_2$ is *not* maximised at the point C.

5. Reading and Exercises

Exercise 1
Consider the constraints of the exercise of Lecture 2.

(a) Graphically determine the point that maximises $x_1 + 2x_2$. Algebraically determine the values of the variables, show that the point is an extreme point and that it is optimal, and determine the value of the objective function.

(b) Graphically determine the point that minimises $x_1 + 2x_2$. Algebraically determine the values of the variables, show that the point is an extreme point and that it is optimal, and determine the value of the objective function.

(c) Graphically determine the point that maximises $2x_1 - x_2$. Algebraically determine the values of the variables, show that the point is an extreme point and that it is optimal, and determine the value of the objective function.

Exercise 2
Consider the resource constraints

$$x_1 - 2x_2 + 3x_3 \leq 30$$

$$2x_1 - 4x_2 + 5x_3 \leq 40$$

$$3x_1 - 4x_2 + 5x_3 \leq 45$$

$$x_1, x_2, x_3 \geq 0.$$

Calculate the point where the first three constraints intersect. Construct an objective function that reaches its optimum at the intersection of the three constraints such that the objective function coefficient of the first decision variable is 3 and the value of the objective function at the optimum is 57.5. How many objective functions that fulfil these criteria are there?

Exercise 3
Consider the Linear Programming problem

$$\text{maximise } 3x_1 + 3x_2$$

$$\text{s. t.} \quad \begin{aligned} x_1 + x_2 &\leq 5 \\ 2x_1 - x_2 &\leq 5 \\ x_2 &\leq 3 \\ x_1, x_2 &\geq 0. \end{aligned}$$

Show that all points between the intersection of the first two constraints and the intersection of the first and the third constraints are optimal solutions.

Exercise 4
An organisation makes a product by blending oils. Each week it wishes to manufacture K tonnes of the final product. Next week there are n oils available as raw materials. A tonne of oil j costs c_j and has hardness h_j. The oils blend linearly; the hardness of the final product must be $\geq \alpha$ and $\leq \beta$. The organisation wishes to determine which oils to use in the blend as to minimise the cost of the final product. Formulate algebraically the firm's problem.

Reading: see Lecture 2.

OR 428 – Model Building in Mathematical Programming

Lecture 4: Linear Programming III - Optimality and Solving LPs

Outline:

1. Optimality II – General Statement
1.1 Optimality conditions for maximisation
1.2 Basic variables, effective constraints, dual variables and optimality conditions
1.3 Maximisation optimality conditions for the cases of ' ≥ ' and '=' constraints
2. Summary: feasibility and optimality conditions for maximisation problems in standard form
3. Example
4. Solving Linear Programming problems
5. Reading and exercises

1. Optimality II - General Statement

1.1 Optimality conditions for maximisation

We have seen in Lecture 3 that we can prove that a certain extreme point is optimal if and only if the objective function can be represented as the weighed sum (with non-negative weights) of the inequalities that define this extreme point. In this lecture we will develop a general statement for the optimality conditions.

Consider the following LP problem in maximisation standard form, with n decision variables and m constraints:

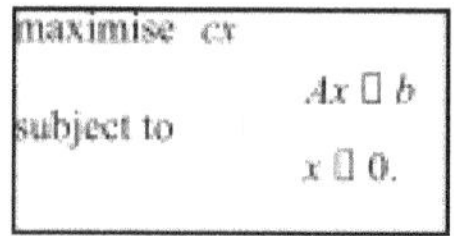

A point x^* is **basic**, if and only if it is the point of intersection of n **linearly independent equalities** which define constraints of the feasible region of the above problem.

We may identify (or define) a basic point x^* by arbitrarily choosing n constraints to be satisfied as equalities, such that the n equalities are linearly independent (no single one can be derived as a weighted combination of the others, using positive or negative weights). These constraints will be referred to as the **defining constraints** for point x^*. Note that there does not necessarily exist a unique set of n defining constraints for any basic point x^*, in which case x^* will be called **degenerate**. Some of the n equalities can be chosen to be resource constraints, i.e. $a_i x^* = b_i$ for some $i \in \{1,2,..., m\}$, while others are will be chosen to be non-negativities, i.e. $x_j^* = 0$ for some components of x^* with $j \in \{1,2,..., n\}$. Note that we may also choose all defining equalities to be resource constraints, or all to be non-negativities.

If and only if a basic point x^* is also **feasible**, i.e. $Ax^* \leq b$ and $x^* \geq 0$, then it is an **extreme point** and hence a candidate for the optimum.

For an extreme point x^* to be **optimal**, we must be able to identify (for at least one way to define x^* if it is degenerate) an $(m + n)$-dimensional vector $[y, w]$, with components y_i ($i \in \{1,2,..., m\}$), one for each resource constraint, and w_j ($j \in \{1,2,..., n\}$), one for each non-negativity, such that:

a) n of the components of $[y, w]$ are non-negative, namely those which correspond to the n constraints that jointly define the basic point x^*.
b) the remaining m of the components of $[y, w]$ are equal to zero
c) we can derive the inequality

$$cx \leq \gamma,$$

where $\gamma = cx^*$ is the objective value at point x^*, as a valid inequality by combining the constraints of the problem using the vector $[y, w]$ as follows:

$$[y \mid w]\begin{bmatrix} A \\ -I \end{bmatrix} x \leq [y \mid w]\begin{bmatrix} b \\ 0 \end{bmatrix}$$

$$\Leftrightarrow (yA - w)x \leq yb,$$

such that $yA = c$ and $yb = \gamma$.

Hence, to check the optimality of an extreme point x^* we have to verify the existence of a solution to the following system of equalities:

$$yA - w = c,$$

with the added conditions that $y_i \geq 0$ for all $i \in \{1,2,..., m\}$ for which the constraint $a_i x^* = b_i$ defines the extreme point; $w_j \geq 0$ for all $j \in \{1,2,..., n\}$ for which the non-negativity $x_j = 0$ defines the extreme point; and all other components of $[y \mid w]$ are equal to 0.

If and only if this is possible (for at least one way to define x^* in the case of a degenerate extreme point), then we have derived the new inequality $cx \leq \gamma^* = yb$, which is the optimal contour of the objective function and satisfies the point x^* as an equality, i.e. the objective function is maximised at x^* and the value of the objective function is $cx^* = \gamma^* = yb$.

Note that by setting, $y_i = 0$, $w_j = 0$ for all non-defining constraints, the above system of equations becomes uniquely determined (defining equalities for a basic point are chosen to be linearly independent). Note also that if x^* is degenerate, then failure to demonstrate optimality using one set of defining constraints does not necessarily imply that the point is not optimal. To conclude with certainty that a degenerate extreme point x^* is not optimal we would have to verify that no appropriate vector $[y \mid w]$ can be constructed for every possible way to define x^*. On the other hand, the

x^* suffices to existence of an appropriate $[y \mid w]$ for at least one way to define establish its optimality.

1.2 Basic/non-basic variables, effective/ineffective constraints, dual variables and maximisation optimality conditions

We will now introduce some new terminology and reformulate the optimality conditions. Apart from the fact that the terminology is helpful as such for talking about an LP problem, we will use the relations derived here for analysing the solution of such problems at a later stage.

Definition:
Consider the general form of a Linear Programming maximisation problem with m resource constraints and n decision variables and non-negativities. For every extreme point, we have (at least) n constraints that are satisfied as equalities. For a given collection of n constraints that define an extreme point, we partition the variables and constraints as follows:

(a) Resource constraints that are satisfied as equalities are called **effective constraints**. All other resource constraints are called **ineffective constraints**.

(b) If a non-negativity contributes to the definition of that point, i.e. $x_j = 0$ for some $j \in \{1,2,..., n\}$, we call the variable x_j a **non-basic variable**, and the other variables are called **basic variables**.

For a **degenerate** extreme point, there will exist multiple ways to partition the variables and constraints as above. In the remainder of this section, we shall consider a **non-degenerate** extreme point.

Note that
the number of basic variables = the number of effective constraints
because we have n decision variables and therefore need n constraints to define the extreme point. Among these constraints, some are non-negativities and some are effective constraints, and *both* the number of contributing non-negativities and effective constraints *and* the number of basic and non-basic variables add up to n.

Let us now have a look at the optimality conditions that are related to these two types of resource constraints and these two types of variables.
Regarding (in-)effective constraints, we have seen above that optimality requires and implies that:

$y_i \geq 0$ for all **effective** constraints, and

$y_i = 0$ (*) for all **ineffective** constraints.

(*)

At the point of optimality, we have $x_j = 0$ for all non-basic variables and $w_j \geq 0$.

Therefore the optimality condition $yA - w = c$, i.e.:

$$ya._j - w_j = c_j ,$$

when we just consider one row of the system, yields for a **non-basic variable**:

$$ya._j \geq c_j. \qquad (*)$$

Regarding basic variables, the non-negativity does not contribute to defining the extreme point. Accordingly, we have $w_j = 0$ at the point of optimality. Hence the optimality condition

$$ya._j - w_j = c_j$$

for the row of a **basic variable** yields

$$ya._j = c_j. \qquad (*)$$

Therefore we have now shown that the optimality conditions given in section 1.1 imply the four statements marked by (*) above. In order to show that these four statements are *equivalent* to the optimality conditions of section 1.1 of this lecture we have to show that these statements collectively imply the optimality conditions of section 1.1.

Consider a vector y which satisfies all four (*) statements and then define, for all j, $w_j = ya._j - c_j$, which means that $w_j \geq 0$ for non-basic variables and $w_j = 0$ for basic variables. It follows directly that the vector $[y \mid w]$ satisfies:

$$ya._j - w_j = c_j \text{ for all } j \in \{1,2,\ldots, n\},$$

which is equivalent to the following of the optimality conditions given in section 1.1:

$$yA - w = c,$$

but it also follows that :

$$[y \mid w] \geq 0,$$

i.e. the vector is non-negative in every component.

Now it remains to show that the m components of the vector $[y \mid w]$ which correspond to constraints that do not contribute to the definition of the extreme point are set equal to zero. This is also almost immediate. Let the number of effective constraints be denoted by e. It follows from the first two (*) statements that out of the m components of the vector y, the number of components which are equal to zero by assumption is m-e, and these in fact correspond to the ineffective resource constraints. Also, by construction of the n-dimensional vector w it follows that the components which correspond to the basic variables, and hence also to the defining non-negativities, are set to zero. Since the number of effective constraints is equal to the number of basic variables, this means that e (out of the n) of the components of vector w are set equal to zero. Therefore, the components of the vector $[y \mid w]$ that are set to zero do in fact correspond to the constraints that define the extreme point under consideration and the number of them is equal to m-e+e=m as required.

In sum we have found another way of expressing the optimality conditions. It has turned out that for verifying optimality of an extreme point, the values of the weights for the non-negativities w_j are not (explicitly) important; all relevant information about the question of whether a certain extreme point is optimal is given by the values of the variables y_i. The relevance of the variables y_i justifies giving them a specific name (the reason for this name will become apparent in a later lecture).

Definition: The above variables y_i ($i \in \{1,2,..., m\}$), i.e. the weights of the resource constraints at the optimum x^*, are called **dual variables**.

1.3 Maximisation optimality conditions for the cases of '≥' and '=' constraints

The optimality conditions that we derived were based on the assumption that the Linear Programming problem is written in the maximisation standard form used above, i.e. with resource constraints that take the form

$$a_i x^* \leq b_i .$$

In most practical applications, however, it makes sense to write the resource constraints in a way that is more appropriate and intuitive in view of our interpretation of the problem. In these cases, we will often use '≥' and '=' constraints, which in principle could be transformed into the standard notation, of course, but are preferred in the non-standard way because they lead to a more transparent model.

Now, as we will see in a subsequent lecture, the values y_i are not only theoretically relevant, but also important for analysing the solution of a Linear Programming problem. Because of this, we will have a quick look at what these values look like at the optimal solution when the constraint has not been written in standard notation.

'≥'- constraints

The area defined by

$$x_1 + 3x_2 \leq 12$$

is the same area that is defined by

$$-x_1 - 3x_2 \geq -12,$$

i.e. by multiplying the coefficients by -1 and reversing the sign of the inequality. In Lecture 3 we found non-negative weights to multiply two constraints to derive the objective function. These were

$$2.6 * (x_1 + 3x_2 \leq 12)$$

$$+ 0.2 * (-3x_1 + x_2 \leq 0)$$

$$= 2x_1 + 8x_2 \leq 31.2$$

Now

$$2.6 *(x_1 + 3x_2 \leq 12)$$

is the same as

$$- 2.6 *(-x_1 - 3x_2 \geq -12).$$

This example shows if the constraint is a '≥' constraint we need *non-positive* weight, that is $y_i \leq 0$, to prove that the point is the optimum.

'='-constraints

The area defined by

$$x_1 + x_2 = 6$$

is the same area that is defined by

$$-x_1 - x_2 = -6$$

that is, multiplying by -1 and making no changes to the sign of the equality. Thus if the optimum point is defined by an equality constraint, to prove optimality the weight y_i can be either sign. The weight of an equality constraint is *free*, it can be any value: negative, zero, or positive.

2. Summary: feasibility and optimality conditions for maximisation problems standard form

Consider the standard problem

$$\text{maximise} \quad cx$$

$$\text{subject to} \quad \begin{array}{l} Ax \le b \\ x \ge 0 \end{array}$$

with n decision variables and m constraints.

A basic point x^* is **feasible** (and so also an extreme point) if and only if we have:

(F1)	$a_i.x^* = b_i$	for all **effective** constraints,
(F2)	$a_i.x^* \le b_i$	for all **ineffective** constraints,
(F3)	$x_j^* \ge 0$	for all **basic** variables, and f
(F4)	$x_j^* = 0$	

orallnon-basicvariables.

The extreme point x^* is **optimal** if and only if there exists a vector y^* such that

(O1)	$y^*a. = c$	for all **basic** variables,
(O2)	$y^*a. \geq c$	for all **non-basic** variables,
(O3)	$y^* \geq 0$	for all **effective** constraints, and
(O4)	$y^* = 0$	for all **ineffective** resource constraints.

Then the objective function is maximised with $\gamma^* = cx^* = y^*b$.

If the basic point x^* is degenerate, then the above will need to hold for at least one way to for at least one way to define x^* .

It is remarkable that the feasibility and optimality conditions look very similar, and there is a great symmetry in the structure of these conditions. This observation leads directly into the theory of Linear Programming *Duality*, which is important for analysing the solution of a Linear Programming problem and will be addressed in a later lecture.

3. Example

Consider the following general maximising LP problem:

$$\begin{aligned} \max \quad & x_1 + 2x_2 \\ \text{subject to} \quad & x_2 \leq 4 \\ & x_1 + x_2 \leq 4 \\ & -x_1 + x_2 \geq -1 \\ & x_1 \geq 0 \\ & x_2 \geq 0 . \end{aligned}$$

Let A denote the coefficient matrix, b the right hand sides vector and c the objective vector, i.e.:

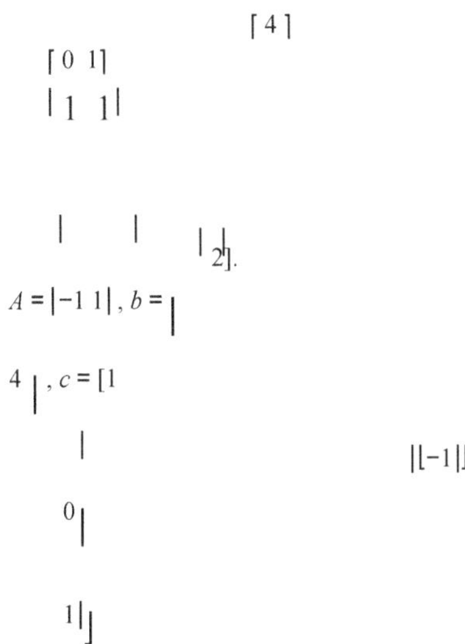

We can construct a basic point by arbitrarily choosing n=2 linearly independent constraints to be satisfied simultaneously as equalities. Let x^A denote the basic point defined by the second and third resource constraints $x_1 + x_2 \le 4$ and $-x_1 + x_2 \ge -1$, i.e. defined as the intersection of these constraints when they are satisfied as equalities. Since no non-negativity is required to define the point, no variable is non-basic, i.e. all variables are basic. We can compute x^A by solving a system of linear equations defined by considering the columns of basic variables and the rows of the effective constraints in the coefficient matrix and the right hand side vector as follows:

$$\begin{bmatrix} 1 & 1 \\ -1 & 1 \end{bmatrix} \begin{bmatrix} x_1^A \\ x_2^A \end{bmatrix} = \begin{bmatrix} 4 \\ -1 \end{bmatrix}$$

$$\Rightarrow x^A = (x_1^A, x_2^A) = (2.5, 1.5) .$$

For x^A to be an extreme point it needs to be feasible. We may verify its feasibility by checking that it satisfies all non-defining constraints (by construction it satisfies the defining constraints). The non-negativities are obviously satisfied and we can check that the ineffective resource constraint is also satisfied by substituting $(x_1^A = 2.5, x_2^A = 1.5)$ to get $1.5 \le 4$.

Since x^A is both basic and feasible, it is an extreme point and hence a candidate for the optimum. To check the optimality of x^A we construct the vector of dual values $y^A = (0, y_2^A, y_3^A)$ (setting $y_1^A = 0$ because the first constraint is ineffective). This vector is determined uniquely by the following system of linear equations:

$$\begin{bmatrix} y_2^A & y_3^A \end{bmatrix} \begin{bmatrix} 1 & 1 \\ -1 & 1 \end{bmatrix} = \begin{bmatrix} 1 & 2 \end{bmatrix}$$

$$\Rightarrow y^A = (y_2^A, y_3^A) = (1.5, 0.5) .$$

For x^A to be an optimal point, the dual vector $y^A = (y_2^A, y_3^A)$ must satisfy conditions: Optimality conditions are violated by $y_3^A = 0.5 \geq 0$ (note that the 3rd constraint is of $\geq$ sign). Therefore, the optimality conditions are not collectively satisfied and so we have not proved optimality for x^A.

Does that necessarily imply that the extreme point x^A is definitely not an optimal point? The answer is "NO"! It could be the case that x^A is a degenerate point and if so another way to define x^A might provide us with a different dual vector that does satisfy all optimality conditions. Thus, for a degenerate point to be declared non optimal, we would need to establish that none of its definitions provides us with a dual vector that satisfies the optimality criteria.

Recall that a point is degenerate if it satisfies more than n inequalities of the LP problem as equalities, where n is the number of variables. By substituting the values into all resource constraints and non-negativities we can of $(x_1^A, x_2^A) = (2.5, 1.5)$ verify that exactly two of them are satisfied as equalities (the second and third resource constraints, which we used to define the point in the first place). Thus, point x^A is not degenerate and so there exists no alternative way to define x^A other than the one we just explored, for which the associated dual vector y^A did not satisfy all optimality conditions. Hence, we can now conclude with certainty that x^A is not an optimal point.

We now proceed to examine another basic point, denoted x^B, which we define by arbitrarily choosing another set of two linearly independent inequalities of the LP problem, namely first resource constraint $x_2 \le 4$ and the first non negativity $x_1 \ge 0$. To determine the (very obvious) values for the variables we solve the following system:

$$\begin{bmatrix} 0 & 1 \\ 1 & 0 \end{bmatrix} \begin{bmatrix} x_1^B \\ x_2^B \end{bmatrix} = \begin{bmatrix} 4 \\ 0 \end{bmatrix}$$

$$\Rightarrow x^B = (x_1^B, x_2^B) = (0, 4).$$

By substituting these values into the constraints of the LP problem we can easily verify that x^B is a feasible basic point, hence an extreme point and a candidate for the optimum. Notice, however that x^B satisfies more than n=2 inequalities as equalities, namely the three inequalities: $x_2 \le 4$, $x_1 + x_2 \le 4$ and $x_1 \ge 0$. Therefore, the point x^B is degenerate extreme point for which there are three equivalent ways to define it by choosing any of the following three pairs of defining constraints: (a) $\{ x_2 \le 4, x_1 \ge 0 \}$, (b) $\{ x_2 \le 4, x_1 + x_2 \le 4 \}$, (c) $\{ x_1 + x_2 \le 4, x_1 \ge 0 \}$.

According to the first of the three pairs (currently under consideration), x_2 is the only basic variable. We may use this definition to calculate that dual value for the effective constraint as $y_1^B = 2$ (all other dual values are set to zero). The dual value $y_1^B = 2 \ge 0$ is of the appropriate sign according to the optimality conditions. However substituting $y_1^B = 2$ into optimality condition regarding the non-basic variable x_1^B gives a violation: $y^* a_{.1} \ge c_1 \Rightarrow 2*0 + 0*1 + 0*(-1) = 0 \le 1$. Hence, we cannot establish optimality of x^B by using the definition in pair (a) above.

We continue with trying to check whether x^B is optimal. We now arbitrarily choose a different defining pair of constraints for x^B, namely pair (b) $\{ x_2 \le 4, x_1 + x_2 \le 4 \}$.

According to this definition, both variables x_1 and x_2 are basic. We now construct the vector of dual values $y^B = (y_1^B, y_2^B, 0)$ which is determined uniquely by the following system of linear equations:

$$\begin{bmatrix} y_1^B & y_2^B \end{bmatrix} \begin{bmatrix} 0 & 1 \\ 1 & 1 \end{bmatrix} = \begin{bmatrix} 1 & 2 \end{bmatrix}$$

$$\Rightarrow y^B = (y_1^B, y_2^B) = (1, 1).$$

Both of the dual values $y_1^B = y_1^B = 1 \geq 0$ are of the appropriate sign according to the optimality conditions. Since there are no non-basic variables, there are no more conditions to check. Thus all of the optimality conditions are satisfied and we can establish with certainty that the point is optimal.

4. Solving Linear Programming problems

The preceding example demonstrated a very rudimentary way for solving LP problems. We now give a general description of the approach that we followed, tailored for maximisation problems in standard form.

In principle, we can use our feasibility and optimality conditions for finding a solution to a LP problem by checking out all basic points according to the following steps:

1. Declare some resource constraints effective constraints, i.e. fulfil (F1).
2. Declare some variables non-basic variables by setting them to zero (F4) such that the system of linear equations given by the (F1) and (F4) has a unique solution x^*, i.e. x^* is a basic point.
3. Check (F2) and (F3). If they are not fulfilled, go back to step 1 and check a different basic point (or possibly the same basic point again in the degenerate case). Otherwise we have an extreme point, with which we proceed.
4. Set the dual values of all ineffective constraints to zero (O4).
5. Solve the system of linear equations given by (O1) and (O4).
6. Check (O2) and (O3). If they are fulfilled, x^* is an optimal solution with

$\gamma^* = cx^* = y^*b$. Otherwise back to step 1 and check the new basic point (or possibly the same basic point using an alternative definition for it in the case of degeneracy).

While carrying out these steps is possible in principle, it would normally need an almost astronomical number of steps (and hence take a very long time) because Linear Programming problems have a large amount of basic points. Fortunately, however, we are not required to check too many basic points. This is due to two properties of Linear Programming problems. For understanding the first property, we need the concept of local and global maxima, for which we will give a definition (in non-mathematical terms) now.

Definition: For a function given by $y = f(x)$, a point x is called a *local maximum* of f if there exists an interval around x in which there is no point with a higher y-value than x. A local maximum is called a *global maximum* of f if the function f has no other local maximum with a higher y-value.

Property 1: When maximising a linear function (the objective function is a linear function) over a convex set (remember the feasible region is a convex set), every local maximum is a global maximum.

This property implies that whenever an extreme point turns out not to be optimal, we can move to any extreme point that has at least the same objective function value – without ever reaching a 'dead-end'.

Property 2: Two adjacent extreme points of the polyhedron (i.e. extreme points that are connected by an edge on the surface of the polyhedron), differ only with respect to one of the variables that are basic.

This property, seen in conjunction with the first property, implies that it is sufficient to walk along the edges of the polyhedron (the feasible region) such that the objective function value does not decrease, and we will finally come to an extreme point that is the optimal solution.

As a consequence, a shorter algorithm is:
1. Start with an extreme point according to (F1), (F2), (F3), (F4).
2. Check optimality according to (O1), (O2), (O3), (O4).
3. If the extreme point is not optimal, move to an adjacent extreme point with a better value of the objective function, and go back to step 2.

(Very, very) roughly speaking, this is the procedure that the most famous algorithm for solving Linear Programming problems, the Simplex Algorithm, carries out. (In its fully developed version, the Simplex Algorithm takes into account many more phenomena, such as: what happens if there is no optimal solution because the problem is unbounded, what happens at extreme points where more than *n* constraints happen to be satisfied as equalities, how to find a first extreme point easily, and how to streamline the algorithm such that it needs as few calculations as possible?)

In the past decades, many variants and specific versions of the Simplex Algorithm have been developed that are very useful for models with a specific structure (the Dual Simplex Algorithm, or the Network Simplex Algorithm, for example), and other, sometimes more efficient algorithms, such as the Interior Point Method, have been invented. As we, in this lecture, are primarily interested in the practical application of Mathematical Programming methods, these few remarks must suffice here. (These and related topics are covered in OR406, however.)

5. Reading and exercises

Exercise 1

Consider the problem:

maximise $-x_1 + 7x_2 + x_3$

subject to $2x_1 + x_2 + x_3 = 5$

x

1 − x 2 + x 3 ≤ 1 4 x 1 − 3 x

2 − x 3 ≥ 0 x 1 , x 2 , x 3 ≥ 0

(a) Show that the point (x_1, x_2, x_3) =(1.5, 2, 0) is feasible and optimal.

(b) If a fourth variable x_4 with technological coefficients 1, 5, 1 in constraints 1, 2 and 3, respectively, and an objective function coefficient of 10 were to be added, would the point (x_1, x_2, x_3, x_4) = (1.5, 2, 0, 0) be optimal?

Exercise 2

Show on the basis of the way in which we developed the optimality conditions for maximisation problems what the optimality conditions for minimisation problems are like.

Exercise 3

Consider the following linear program:

minimise $10x_1 + 10x_2 + 6x_3 + 12x_4 - 4x_6$

subject to

$$2x_1 + x_2 + x_3 + x_4 - 3x_5 - x_6 \geq 8$$

$$x_1 + 2x_2 + x_3 + 3x_4 + x_5 - 4x_6 \geq 3$$

$$x_1, x_2, x_3, x_4, x_5, x_6 \geq 0$$

Confirm that $x^* = (4, 0, 0, 0, 0, 0)$ and $y^* = (5, 0)$ is an optimal solution to this program where y^* are the dual values of the resource constraints.

Reading

Required: ---
Recommended: You can read more about the Simplex Method in chapters 4.1. to 4.3 of Hillier, F.S. and Liebermann, G.J. (2001).
Suggested: You will find a more theoretical treatment of optimality in chapters 2.6 and 3.1 of Bertsimas, D. and Tsitsiklis, J.N. (1997); the fundamentals of the Simplex Method are covered in chapters 3.2 and 3.3.

OR428 – Model Building in Mathematical Programming

Lecture 5: Modelling Environments I - The Modelling Life Cycle and How Modelling Environments Function

Outline:

1. The Modelling Life Cycle
2. Why do we need Modelling Environments?
3. Technical Terms related to Modelling Environments
4. How Modelling Environments function
5. Reading and exercises

1. The Modelling Life Cycle (including the use of computers)

Until now we have considered only very small models where we could have found the optimum by just checking all basic points. However, a model with n variables and m (independent) constraints has $\frac{(n+m)!}{n!\,m!}$ basic points. Accordingly, even a rather small model with 100 variables and 100 constraints has around $9 * 10^{58}$ basic points, and a model with 1000 variables and 1000 constraints features around $2 * 10^{600}$ basic points (compare this with the approx. $1.8 * 10^{20}$ seconds that have passed since the big bang, or the number of stars in the universe, which has been estimated to be $7 * 10^{22}$.) Real-life problems can easily have 1,000,000 variables and constraints. Under these circumstances, even if we do not check all basic points for optimality and apply an intelligent algorithm like the Simplex Algorithm for solving a model, we will still have far too many basic points to be able to check them manually. In other words: using a computer for solving most practical Linear Programming problems is indispensable.

The following diagram illustrates the process of using mathematical model(s) for solving a decision problem.

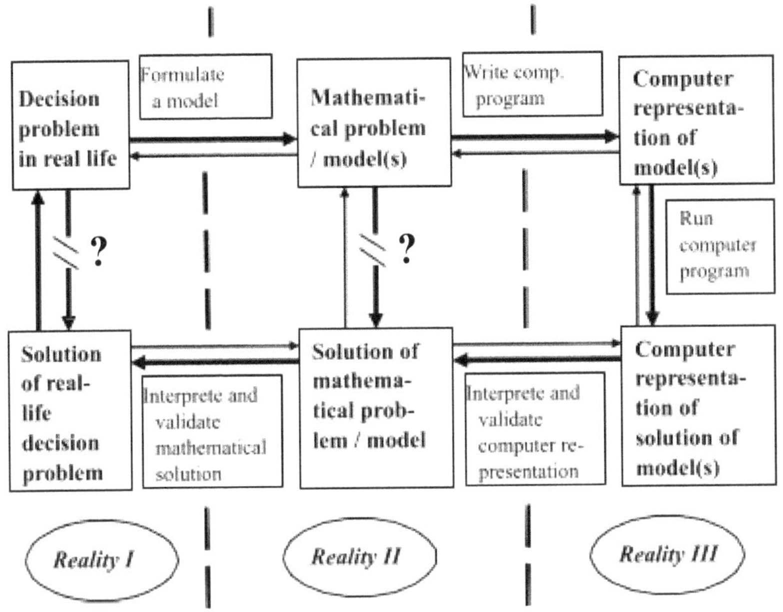

Remarks:

1. When relying on computer support for solving a mathematical model, it is important to distinguish three separate levels ("realities") of the problem: the real-life problem, the mathematical problem, and the computer programming problem. While for small models the computer representation of the model will probably not pose any significant additional problems (because computer programming languages have very much in common with formal mathematical descriptions of a problem), representing large models on a computer can lead to major difficulties. In cases where the computer representation of the mathematical model(s) consists of several thousand lines of programme code, for example, it is necessary not to assume too readily that the computer representation actually corresponds to the mathematical model.

2. Note that the process of modelling is illustrated by a cycle (Modelling Life Cycle, see thick arrows) – or, rather, in our case, by two overlapping cycles. The iterative, non-linear nature of this process is due to the fact that using mathematical models involves an ongoing process of learning about the decision problem, the mathematical model, and the computer representation of the model.

3. Note the thin arrows in the diagram. They indicate that every step through the modelling life cycle should involve frequent (independent) checks, double-checks, triple-checks and cross-checks with regard to the relations between all three levels of reality.

(For further aspects of the modelling life cycle see chapter 3 in Huerlimann (1999))

2. Why do we need Modelling Environments?

The time needed for solving a model is not the only reason why computer support is helpful when setting up a Mathematical Programming model. Other reasons are in particular:

1. Formulating the model: Large practical problems, with thousands of variables and constraints, are often not set up by defining an x-vector, an A-matrix and b- and c- vectors (in order to be transparent and manageable). Instead, they are formulated in a way that reflects more closely the way in which the modeller interprets the real decision problem. Typical phenomena in this respect are:

- Different types of variables and coefficients with different names,
- Variables and coefficients can have several indices,
- Indices can be elements of specific sets ("index sets"), which might have a complex structure or are to be generated on the basis of other mathematical models,
- Every component of the constants A, b and c can consist of several coefficients, which have to be calculated before solving the model,
- Combinations of "≤"-constraints, "≥"-constraints and "="-constraints,
- One 'written' constraint can represent many different constraints of a similar structure, each of which is valid with respect to one element from an index set.

If the number of inequalities and the data set is large, it is a tedious and error-prone task to transform a model with these characteristics into input data for a Linear Programming algorithm such as the Simplex Algorithm.

2. Solving collections of interdependent models: In the case of complex practical applications, we often have to solve not just a single Mathematical Programming model, but a collection of models the input data of some of which is based on the output data of others. In such a case we need a way of coordinating models and transferring data between them. Moreover, complex models often require customised algorithms and not just an all-purpose algorithm to solve them.

3. Interpreting the solution of models: Complex decision problems often lead to a large amount of data, i.e. thousands of numbers. Interpreting them is nearly impossible without resorting to computer support.

4. Import and export of data: Complex decision problems can often be modelled only by drawing on large databases, which will be fed with the solution of models in return. Therefore, using Mathematical Programming models successfully calls for a flexible ways in which models and their solutions can be connected with databases or Excel sheets.

5. Tracing errors: Carrying out large modelling projects can lead to significant errors at every stage of the projects. When several thousands of variables and constraints are involved, it is helpful to have computer support for tracing errors.

Modelling environments are software packages that have specifically been designed for addressing these five (and other) problems related to using large scale mathematical models.

3. Technical Terms related to Modelling Environments

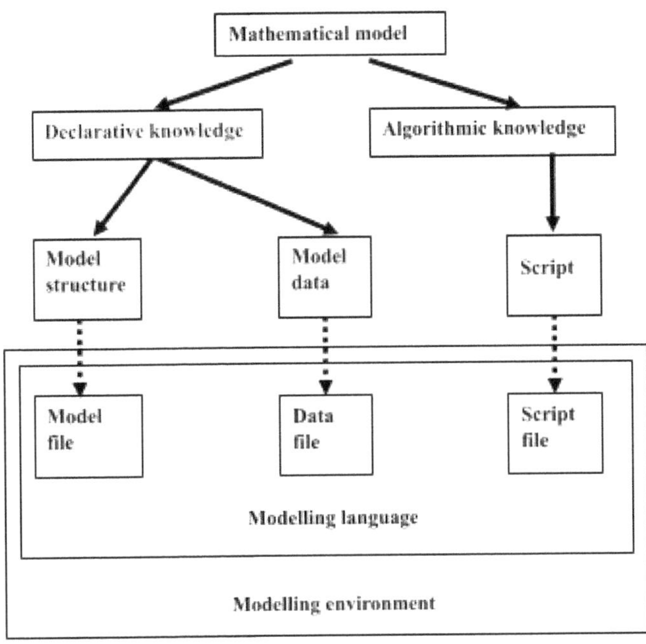

Mathematical model: a mathematical interpretation of a real decision problem that consists of *declarative* and *algorithmic knowledge* and has been built with the pragmatic purpose of supporting the process of finding a solution to the real decision problem. We can distinguish between models of different qualities with respect to the fitness for purpose the model demonstrates.

Modelling language: a computer programming language that allows us to represent a mathematical model. A fully fledged modelling language can express both the *declarative* and the *algorithmic knowledge* of the problem that we have modelled. *AMPL* ('A Mathematical Programming Language') and *OPL* ('Optimisation Programming Language') are among the most powerful modelling languages that are available for Mathematical Programming problems.

Declarative knowledge: the amount of information contained in the interpretation of a real decision problem that is represented in terms of the *model structure* and the *model data* of a *mathematical model* (or a collection of mathematical models).

Model structure: the part of a *mathematical model* that consists only of the general mathematical structure of the problem, i.e. the model without any concrete values of the parameters, index-sets and coefficients, and without the *algorithmic knowledge*.

Model data: the part of a *mathematical model* that consists of the values (numerical or alphanumerical) to be assigned to parameters, coefficients, index sets, and – eventually – variables.

Model instance: a model with concrete data having been assigned to all parameters, index sets and coefficients, i.e. the *model structure* and concrete *model data.*

Matrix generator: a computer programme that transforms a *model instance* of a Mathematical Programming problem that has been represented by means of a *modelling language* into its *algorithmic representation.* In the case of a Linear Programming problem, this means to generate the matrix A and the vectors b and c.

Algorithmic representation: the mathematical standard form of a mathematical problem, which is used by algorithms (*solvers*) to solve this type of problem. In the case of a Linear Programming problem the algorithmic representation consists of the matrix A and the vectors b and c.

Pre-solver: a computer programme that reduces the initial *algorithmic representation* of a problem to an algorithmic representation that can be solved more easily.

Solver: a computer programme that tries to find a *solution* of a *mathematical model* (or a part of a mathematical model). Examples of solvers that can be used within the *modelling environment AMPLDev* are *IpOpt, FortMP* and *CPLEX.*

Solution: an assignment of values to all variables of a *mathematical model* that has the properties the modeller is looking for.

Report generator: a computer programme that displays the *solution* (and data about the solution process) generated by the *solver* such that modellers can easily interpret it against the background of their mathematical model.

Algorithmic knowledge: the amount of information contained in the interpretation of a real decision problem that is represented in an algorithm to solve it. Within a *modelling environment,* algorithmic knowledge is normally represented by a *script* (file).

Script: a way of representing algorithmic knowledge by means of a *modelling language* such as *AMPL* or *OPL.* Scripts written in these modelling languages contain information with respect to specific procedures for *solving* a collection of *model instances,* reorganising data and transferring it between model instances, exporting and importing data from outside the *Modelling environment,* and specific commands for customising the *solver* to the mathematical model at hand.

Modelling environment: a software package that includes, among other features, a graphical user interface and a *modelling language* that enable modellers to represent *mathematical models* by a computer, supports the process of finding a *solution* of the model, and provides means of importing and exporting data and of tracing errors. Examples of fully fledged modelling environments are *AMPLDev* and the *ILOG OPL-CPLEX Development System.*

4. How Modelling Environments work

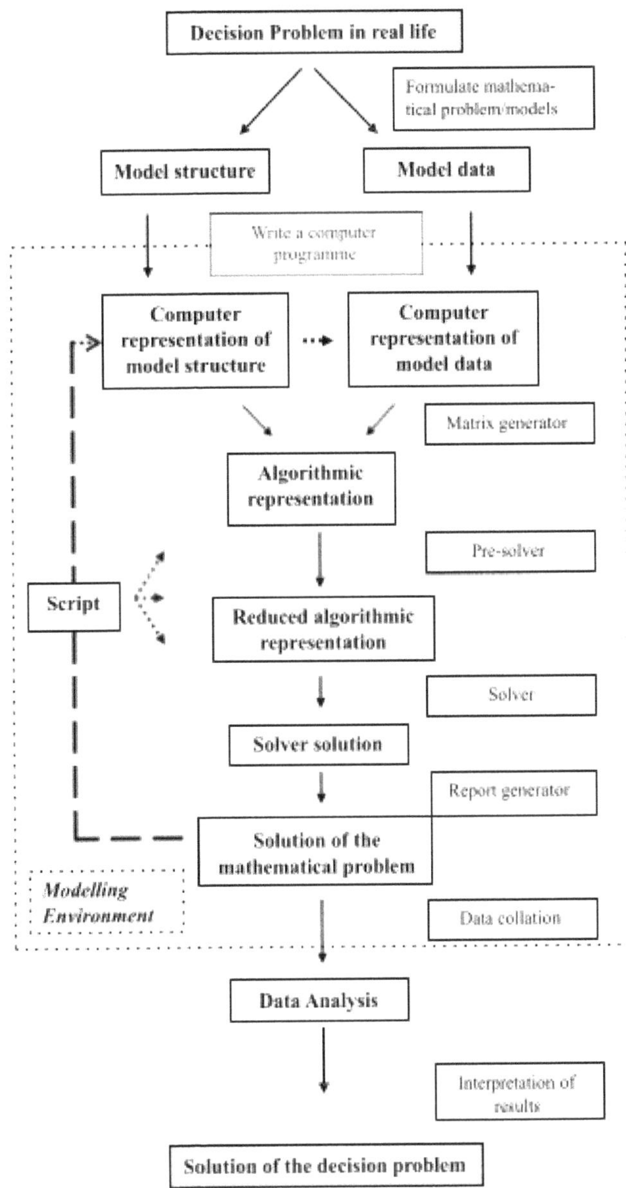

5. Reading and exercises

Exercise 1

Monthly demand for a product is known for the forthcoming months, and this demand must be met. It is possible to store the product from one month to the next. The costs of production in each month and the cost of storage from a month to the next for a unit of product are known. There is unlimited storage space, the initial inventory is known, and no final inventory is required. The plan should cover *T* months. If production changes from a month to the next then there is a penalty cost of per unit in the change in the production level. The penalty per unit is different for an increase and a decrease in production levels.

(a) Formulate algebraically this problem.

(b) Solve the problem using the following data: The plan should cover T=4 months. Production cost in all months is: 10. Storage costs are 6 per unit per month.
Demand in the 4 months is 10, 8, 14, 20 respectively.
The initial inventory is zero.
Penalty for production increase is 4 per unit.
Penalty for production decrease is 3 per unit.

Exercise 2

A certain company has three branch plants with excess production capacity. All three plants have the capability for producing a certain product and so management has decided to use the excess capacity for this purpose. The product can be made in three sizes – large, medium and small – which yield a net unit profit of £12, £10 and £9 respectively. Plants 1, 2 and 3 have excess manpower and equipment capacity which allows them to produce up to 500, 600 and 300 units respectively and this capacity can be used to produce the product in any size or combination of sizes. However, the amount of available in-process storage space also imposes a limitation on the production rates. Plants 1, 2 and 3 have 9000, 8000 and 3500 square meters of in-process storage space available for this product. Each unit of the large, medium and small sizes produced per day requires 20, 15 and 12 square meters respectively.

Sales forecast indicate that up to 600, 800 and 500 units of the large, medium and small sizes, respectively can be sold per day.

In order to maintain a uniform workload among the plants and to retain some flexibility, management has decided that the additional production assigned to each plant must use the same percentage of the excess manpower and equipment capacity.

Management wishes to know how much of each of the sizes should be produced by each of the plants in order to maximise profit.

Exercise 3

An investor has money-making activities A and B available at the beginning of each of the next five years. Each pound invested in A at the beginning of one year returns £1.40 (a profit of £.40) two years later (in time for immediate reinvestment). Each pound invested in B at the beginning of one year returns £1.70 three years later.

In addition, money-making activities C and D will each be available at one time in the future. Each pound invested in C at the beginning of the second year hence returns £2 four years later. Each pound invested in D at the beginning of the fifth year hence returns £1.30 one year later.

The investor begins with £100,000. He wishes to know which investment plan maximizes the amount of money he can accumulate by the beginning of the sixth year hence.

Reading

Required:

- "The Modelling Life Cycle" (chapter 3 in: Huerlimann, T. (1999), pages 37-66), handed out in the lecture. (When reading it, feel free to skip the examples; this text is meant to give you a more detailed general idea of typical problems that can arise when using mathematical models for solving a decision problem.)

[Note: This week you are given two texts as required reading. If you are short of time, please focus on the required reading for Lecture 6 (chapters from the AMPLDev User Manual). You can postpone the Huerlimann for when you have more time available.]

Recommended:

- "Building Linear Programming Models", chapter 3 in Williams (2001), pp 17-38.

Suggested:

- Chapters 1, 2, 4 in Huerlimann, T. (1999)

<u>OR428 – Model Building in Mathematical Programming</u>

Lecture 6: Modelling Environments II – Introduction to AMPLDev, representing the model structure in AMPL

<u>Outline:</u>

1. An example of a production problem
2. How to represent the model structure
2.1 Defining index sets and scalar parameters
2.2 Defining vector parameters
2.3 Defining variables and representing the non-negativities
2.4 Representing the objective function
2.5 Representing the resource constraints
2.6 The complete model file
3. Reading and exercises

1. An example of a production problem

We have used AMPL in a very simple way since Lecture 1. This lecture is meant to increase your understanding of the modelling language AMPL and take your ability to represent Mathematical Programming problems with a computer to a higher, more professional level. Let us start with an example of a production problem, of the basis of which we will introduce new AMPL concepts in sections 2 and 3 of this lecture.

A company manufactures n_K products and has at its disposal n_H machines. It can undertake normal and overtime production and needs to plan for n_I time periods. The products can be stored between periods, but the capacity is limited. Any product left over from the last period must be sold very cheaply. Machine capacities, selling prices, demand for each product, and storage capacities are given. How should the company produce each product in order to fulfil all constraints?

A mathematical interpretation of this problem could look as follows:

Index sets:

$I = \{1,2,..., n_I\}$ the set of time periods

$J = \{normal, overtime\}$ the set of production modes

$K = \{1,2,..., n_K\}$ the set of products

$H = \{1,2,..., n_H\}$ the set of machines

Variables:

- X_{ijkh} units of product k produced on machine h in period i in production mode j (normal or overtime),
- Y_{ik} units of product k stored in period i, $i \in I \cup \{0\}$
- Z_{ik} units of product k sold in period i.

Parameters:

- u_k storage capacity of product k
- r_k final selling price of product k at the end of last period
- a_{ijh} capacity (in hours, for example) of machine h in production mode j in period i
- p_{ik} selling price of product k in period i
- d_{ik} demand of product k in period i
- c_{ijkh} cost to produce one unit of product k on machine h in period i in production mode j
- s_k storage cost per unit of product k
- t_{ijkh} units of capacity consumption (in hours, for example) due to producing one unit of product k on machine h in period i in production mode j

Constraints:

Storing product between periods i:

$$\sum_{j \in J, h \in H} X_{ijkh} + Y_{i-1,k} = Y_{ik} + Z_{ik} \qquad \text{for all } i \in I, k \in K$$

$$Y_{0k} = 0 \qquad \text{for all } k \in K$$

Storage is limited:

$$Y_{ik} \leq u_k \qquad \text{for all } i \in I \setminus \{n_I\}, k \in K$$

Machine capacity is limited:

$$\sum_{k \in K} t_{ijkh} * X_{ijkh} \leq a_{ijh} \qquad \text{for all } i \in I, j \in J, h \in H$$

Demand must be satisfied:

$$Z_{ik} = d_{ik} \qquad \text{for all } i \in I, k \in K$$

Objective function:

maximise

$$\sum_{i\in I, k\in K} p_{ik} * Z_{ik} + \sum_{k\in K} r_k Y_{n_I k} - \sum_{\substack{i\in I, j\in J, k\in K \\ h\in H}} c_{ijkh} * X_{ijkh} - \sum_{k\in K} \left(s_k * \sum_{i\in I\setminus\{n_I\}} Y_{ik}\right)$$

Notice that no index in a constraint must be "left over": either the index is used for a sum or it is used for a "for all"-expression. Similarly, in the objective function all indices must be 'tied' to a sum.

2. How to represent the model structure

In the following, we will go through the model structure of the production problem in a step by step fashion and illustrate the use of AMPL for representing it on a computer.

2.1 Defining index sets and scalar parameters

We will start with the sets. Let us call the index set 'I' that models the time periods 'TIME' in AMPL (we could choose a different name, of course, but this would lead to a less transparent model file). We will denote the final period of time by 'T'. In order to define the set TIME = {1, 2, …, T} in AMPL, we write:

```
set TIME := 1..T;
```

Analogously we define the set of products and the set of machines by

```
set PROD := 1..P;
set MACH := 1..M;
```

However, for AMPL to know what 'T', 'P' and 'M' are, we have to write (before the definitions of these sets):

```
param T;
param P;
param
M;
```

These three lines tell AMPL that T, P and M are scalar parameters (i.e. simple numbers, as opposed to vectors) that will later be assigned numbers on the basis of the data file (that we will write in chapter 3 of this lecture). When combining the model file and the data file to generate the algorithmic representation of a model instance, AMPL will automatically define the sets TIME, PROD and MACH according to the values of T, P and M, respectively, that the data file provides.

The set of production modes is of a different type. In contrast to TIME, PROD and MACH, it does *not* contain numbers, but strings of letters. Such a set is defined in AMPL as follows:

```
set MODE := {"normal", "overtime"};
```

i.e. the strings must be put in quotation marks (otherwise AMPL would not know where the strings end, i.e. that the first string, for example, ends before the comma).

2.2 Defining vector parameters

In a next step we inform AMPL about the vector parameters that we intend to use. In the model above these are the parameters u_k , r_k , a_{ijh} , p_{ik} , d_{ik} , c_{ijkh} , s_k , and t_{ijkh} . In the following, we will keep the names of the parameter as they are used in the mathematical model above, just in order to introduce not too many names of parameters here in our small example. A more professional way of representing an LP problem with a computer, however, consists in choosing names for parameters that are similar to the phenomenon modelled. The "mathematical" style in which the parameters have been given names in the model structure above is not very helpful for long and complex computer programmes. So ' $storeCap_k$ ' would definitely be a better name than u_k for a parameter that models the storage capacity of product k, for example.

Regarding the parameter u_k , we have to tell AMPL that u_k is a parameter, that it is a vector (i.e. that it comes with an index), and that this index is an element of the set PROD. This is achieved as follows:

```
param u {PROD};
```

The same applies to the parameter r_k :

```
param r {PROD};
```

The parameter a_{ijh} has more than one index, namely indices that are elements of the sets TIME, MODE and MACH. Accordingly, we write

```
param a {TIME, MODE, MACH};
```

to give AMPL the necessary information.
Analogously, we define the other parameters:

```
param p {TIME, PROD};
param d {TIME, PROD};
param c {TIME, MODE, PROD, MACH};
param s {PROD};
param t {TIME, MODE, PROD, MACH};
```

Note that the order in which we write the sets within the '{}'-brackets here will be important when we refer to the parameters later. Whenever we wish to refer to the parameter t, for example, we have to keep in mind that – due to the definition we just have written – the first index always refers to the point of time, the second to the mode of production, the third to the product, and the fourth to the type of machine used.
Further note that we are writing only the model structure at the moment. When we have set up the data file for our production problem, AMPL will assign values to the parameter once we tell it to solve the problem.

2.3 Defining variables and representing the non-negativities

We have now reached the point where we will inform AMPL about the variables of our LP problem. Since Lecture 1 we have used only scalar variables. The variables here, however, are vector variables, which is why we write:

```
var X {TIME, MODE, PROD, MACH} >= 0;
var Y {0..T, PROD} >= 0;
var Z {TIME, PROD} >= 0;
```

Note that, for defining the first index of Y_{ik}, we have not drawn on the set TIME. This is the case because the index i of Y_{ik} can also take the value 0, i.e. is an element of the set TIME $\cup$ {0}.

2.4 Representing the objective function

The objective function has four terms. Let us start with the most simple one, namely

$$\sum_{k \in K} r_k Y_{nk} .$$

We have to let AMPL know that we would like to sum up several terms $r_k Y_{nk}$. In AMPL, one component of the vector r_k is referred to as 'r[k]', and analogously Y_{nk} is referred to as 'Y[T, k]' (if we keep in mind that we have decided to use the name 'T' for the last element of the set TIME). The entire sum then reads

```
sum {k in PROD} r[k]*Y[T, k].
```

The first term of the objective function is also a sum, but it runs over more than one index, namely over *two* indices. To represent this in AMPL, we write:

```
sum {i in TIME, k in PROD} p[i, k]*Z[i, k].
```

Analogously we write

```
sum {i in TIME, j in MODE, k in PROD, h in MACH} c[i, j, k, h]*X[i, j, k, h]
```

for the third term of the objective function.

We have called the indices for summation 'i', 'j', 'k', 'h' here. Whenever we use indices within in a sum, AMPL remembers them only as long as we are still dealing with this particular sum. This means that we could use the index 'i' to refer to some elements of TIME in one sum, and could use the index 'j' to refer to the elements of TIME in a different sum. Sometimes this is helpful when we have many sums in our model structure. (A good programmer, however, normally uses *different* indices for the elements of different sets in order to keep the programme transparent.) Indices of this type, which are valid only temporarily within a sum, are called dummy indices.

The fourth term of the objective function features a sum over a product one of the factors of which is another sum. In AMPL we express this as follows:

```
sum {k in PROD} (s[k] * sum {i in TIME} Y[i, k]).
```

Note that the brackets "( )" are not necessary here as, in mathematics, a product has priority over a sum. However, when using programming languages, it is not always clear if they stick to the rules of priority in mathematics. Whenever you are unsure, use too many rather than too few brackets!

The fourth term has one more detail that we have left out above: the second sum does not run over the set TIME, but instead uses the set TIME\{T}. In AMPL, there are two ways of expressing this. One way, the direct way, consists in using set operations. AMPL has four built in set operations, which are

A union B	for the union of A and B,
A inter B	for the intersection of A and B,
A diff B	for the difference of A and B, and
A symdiff B	for the symmetric difference of A and B.

Accordingly, we can write the fourth term of the objective function as

```
sum {k in PROD} (s[k] * sum {i in TIME diff {T}} Y[i, k]).
```

Another option of writing this term is by means of conditional sums. A conditional sum is a sum where the index, in order to take part in the summation, must fulfil a certain condition. In this case, the elements of 'TIME diff {T}' are all indices i that are in TIME *and* fulfil the condition $i < T$. In AMPL this is written as

```
sum {k in PROD} (s[k] * sum {i in TIME: i< T} Y[i, k]).
```

Note that conditional sums, which are very helpful for many models, can also take more complicated forms. If this were relevant for our model, we could use, for example, sums like: sum {k in PROD, i in TIME: r[k] <= 5*d[i,k]} (r[k]*Y[i,k] + s[k]).

All in all, our objective function looks as follows:

```
minimize Profit:
          sum {i in TIME, k in PROD} p[i, k] * Z[i, k]
        + sum {k in PROD} r[k] * Y[T, k]
        -         sum {i in TIME, j in MODE, k in
                  PROD, h in MACH} [i, j, k, h] * X[i, j,
                  k, h]
        - sum {k in PROD} (s[k] * sum {i in TIME: i< T} Y[i, k]).
```

2.5 Representing the resource constraints

In contrast to the simple constraints that we have used since Lecture 1, the constraints in this model are <u>constraints with indices</u>. The constraint that sets the initial stock at zero, for example, reads

$$Y_{0k} = 0 \text{ for all } k \in K .$$

This means that this single equation represents $|K|$ different constraints, one for each element of the set K. In AMPL, we write the set of the indices for which the constraint holds directly after the name of the constraints in "{ }" and use dummy variables (as we would do for a sum). Therefore the initial stock constraint (we will baptise it 'storageIni') is represented by

```
storageIni {k in PROD}: Y[0, k] = 0;
```

Again analogously to sums, we can write the storage balance constraint

$$\sum_{j \in J,\, h \in H} X_{ijkh} + Y_{i-1,k} = Y_{ik} + Z_{ik} \quad \text{for all } i \in I,\ k \in K$$

as

```
storageBal {I in TIME, k in PROD}:
        sum {j in MODE, h in MACH} X [i, j, k, h] + Y [i-1, k]
    = Y [i, k] + Z [i, k];
```

In a similar fashion we can express the constraints for the machine capacity as

```
machineCap {i in TIME, j in MODE, h in MACH}:
        sum {k in PROD} t [i, j, k, h] * X [i, j, k, h]
    <= a [i, j, h];
```

and the demand constraints as

```
demand {i in TIME, k in PROD}:
        Z [i, k] = d [i, k];
```

Not only the indices used for summation, but also the indices used for a constraint can be subject to <u>conditions</u> and <u>set operations</u>. In our model, the upper bound constraint of the storage capacity is subject to such a condition. Analogously to the case of sums, we can write:

```
storageCap {i in (TIME diff {T}), k in PROD}:
        Y [i, k] <= u[k];
```

or, alternatively,

```
storageCap {i in TIME: i < T, k in PROD}:
        Y [i, k] <= u[k];
```

2.6 The complete model file

We can now write the complete model file. When writing a model file it is important that we choose a way of structuring our model by means of comments, i.e. lines (or parts of lines) that begin with the sign '#'. Within every line, AMPL will ignore all symbols that follow the sign '#'. Therefore we are free to make any type of comments within the model file. The specific way in which comments are made is a matter of taste of the individual computer programmer and should depend on both the length and complexity of the model file. In any case, it is important that modellers and computer programmers start to develop their own style of making comments while dealing with small model files. Doing so guarantees that it will be easy for them to adapt the style of their comments once they encounter longer, more complex problems such that also these problems can be represented in a transparent and well-documented fashion.
The way in which comments (and spaces) are used in the following model file should be regarded as the minimum of what is routinely necessary.

```
# Model file name:
# C:\Program Files\AmplStudio Modeling System 1.6.J\Bin\OR428\ #
ProductionProblemLecture6.mod

##############################
###   PARAMETERS,   SETS   ####
##############################

### PARAMETERS: SCALARS ##

# Number of time periods
param T;
# Number of products param
P;
# Number of machines param
M;

### SETS ##################

# Time periods set
TIME := 1..T;
# Production modes
set MODE := {"normal", "overtime"}; #
Products
set PROD := 1..P;
# Machines
set MACH := 1..M;

### PARAMETERS: VECTORS ##

# storage capacity
param u {PROD};
# final cheap selling price
param r {PROD};
# machine capacity
param a {TIME, MODE, MACH};
# selling price
param p {TIME, PROD}; #
demand
param d {TIME, PROD};
```

```
# production cost
param c {TIME, MODE, PROD, MACH};
# storage cost param
s {PROD};
# capacity consumption
param t {TIME, MODE, PROD, MACH};

###########################
# ### VARIABLES        ###
###########################
#

# quantity produced
var X {TIME, MODE, PROD, MACH} >= 0;

# quantity stored
var Y {0 .. T, PROD} >= 0;
# quantity sold
var Z {TIME, PROD} >= 0;

###########################
# ### OBJECTIVE FUNCTION ###
###########################
#
#     Profit
# := revenue due to regular sale # +
revenue due to final sale
# - production cost #
- storage cost

maximize Profit:
#     revenue due to regular sale
      sum {i in TIME, k in PROD} p[i, k] * Z[i, k]

# + revenue due to final sale
    + sum {k in PROD}    r[k]                    * Y[T, k]

# - production cost

  -    sum {i in TIME, j in MODE, k in PROD, h in MACH}
                               c[i, j, k, h] * X[i, j, k, h]

# - storage cost

  -    sum {k in PROD} (s[k] * sum {i in TIME: i < T} Y[i, k]);

#########################
# ### CONSTRAINTS    ###
#########################
#

subject to

# storage balance
storageBal {i in TIME, k in PROD}:
    sum {j in MODE, h in MACH} X[i, j, k, h]
   + Y [i-1, k]
   = Y [i,   k]
   + Z [i,   k];

# storage initialisation
storageIni {k in PROD}:
    Y [0,   k] = 0;

# storage capacity
storageCap {i in (TIME diff {T}), k in PROD}: Y
    [i, k] <= u[k];
```

```
# machine capacity
machineCap {i in TIME, j in MODE, h in MACH}: sum {k in
    PROD} t[i, j, k, h] * X[i, j, k, h]
 <= a[i, j, h];

# demand to be satisfied demand
{i in TIME, k in PROD}:
     Z [i, k] = d [i, k];
```

3. Reading and exercises

Exercise 1

A manufacturer of Bits and Bobs wishes to schedule his production to minimize cost 2 months in advance. The only costs which vary are the labour cost and storage cost. The firm works a 40 hour week with 5 employees, paid £2 per hour. They will work up to 10 hours overtime at "time-and-a-half" rates. Bits require 7 man-hours per thousand units, and Bobs require 16.25 man-hours per thousand units. The demand in thousand units that must be met over the next two months is as follows:

	Bits	Bobs
Month 1	40	24
Month 2	20	56

(You may assume that no units are required beyond month 2, and that a "month" is exactly 4 weeks.)

It costs £5 to store a thousand Bits produced in month 1 for sale in month 2, and £8 for Bobs.

Formulate an LP problem to determine the manufacturer's optimal production plan, that satisfies demand at minimum total cost.

Exercise 2 (generalised version of Exercise 1)

Consider a firm making a set of products. The monthly demand for these products in the next months is known and must be met. It is possible to store each product from one month to the next, and there is no limit on storage. The firm utilises labour in different work-modes (e.g. normal time and overtime), and employs sufficient people so that each month there is a fixed number of available man-hours for all working modes. The only costs which vary are the labour and storage costs. The costs of storage varies across products but is the same across all months. The wages per man-hour vary across work-modes but are also fixed across months.

Write the model structure of and programme the model file in AMPL.

Exercise 3

A student has 10 weeks to prepare for an examination in 3 papers. His "grade average", which he wishes to maximise, is the average of his marks (percentage) on the 3 papers, but he will fail the examination altogether if he has been less than 40% on any one paper.

He estimates that without any further study he would obtain 20% on paper I, 60% on paper II, and 30% on paper III. He also estimates that he can improve his marks by devoting time to the various papers at the rate of 5 marks per week on paper I, 10 marks per week on II, and 8 marks per week on III. But he is certain that no amount of study can raise his mark on any paper above 80%.

a) Advise the student on how to distribute his remaining time before the exam. What is his expected grade?

b) The rules for assessment of the exam have been tightened up by the additional restriction that the student's grade will not be more than 15 marks higher than the lowest mark of the three papers. Revise your advice to the student.

Reading:

Required: Chapters 4, 5 and 6 from the AMPLDev User Manual by OptiRisk Systems (available on Moodle)

Recommended: Have a look at "AMPL : a modeling language for mathematical programming" by Robert Fourer, David M. Gay, and Brian W. Kernighan (2003), who are the creators of AMPL (available in the library), and read chapters that you think will be helpful.

Suggested: --

OR428 – Model Building in Mathematical Programming

Lecture 7: Modelling Environments III – Representing the model data in AMPL

Outline:

1. How to represent the model data
1.1 Defining the values of scalar parameters and sets
1.2 Defining the values of vector parameters
1.3 The complete data file
2. Reading and exercises

1. How to represent the model data

The model data is represented by a data file. In the case of our production problem, this means that we have to write a file that assigns values to the scalar parameters and the vector parameters (the sets are implicitly defined by the scalar parameters).

1.1 Defining the values of scalar parameters and sets

The data for the three scalar parameters T, P and M can be provided in a straight forward way:

```
param T := 2;
param P := 3;
param M := 3;
```

Note that with these three lines, we have *implicitly* defined the sets 'TIME', 'PROD' and 'MACH' as follows:

```
TIME := {1, 2}
PROD := {1, 2, 3}
MACH := {1, 2, 3}.
```

We have defined the set MODE within the AMPL model file by using the statement

```
set MODE := {"normal", "overtime"};
```

If you would like to define the same set within an AMPL data file (which is not necessary here because we have already defined it in the model file) the statement would have to be:

```
set MODE := normal overtime;
```

that is without brackets and quotation marks. So the syntax of AMPL data files is slightly different form AMPL model files.)

1.2 Defining the values of vector parameters

In the case of vector parameters, i.e. parameters with indices, we have to take into account the number of indices. A parameter with one index is assigned values in the form of a list. Let us have a look at the parameter 'u {PROD}' in the computer representation, i.e. the parameter u_k in the mathematical model, which, in AMPL, is assigned values as follows:

```
param u :=   1     20
             2     20
             3      0;
```

The first column of this list contains the different values of the index, i.e. in this case it contains all elements of the set PROD. The second column contains the values of the different components of the parameter. In mathematical notation, the definition above is equivalent to

$$(u_1, u_2, u_3) := (20,20,0) .$$

A parameter with two indices is assigned values in the form of a table. As it is the case with matrices in mathematics, the first index of the parameter refers to the rows of the table, while the second index refers to its columns. Regarding the parameter 'd{TIME, PROD}' which models the demand, we write:

```
param d :        1     2     3    :=
           1    25    30    30
           2    30    25    25;
```

which in AMPL represents the mathematical statement

$$\begin{pmatrix} d_{11} & d_{12} & d_{13} \\ d_{21} & d_{22} & d_{23} \end{pmatrix} := \begin{pmatrix} 25 & 30 & 30 \\ 30 & 25 & 25 \end{pmatrix} .$$

For parameters with three indices, there is the problem that we have to find a way to represent a three-dimensional assignment on a two-dimensional computer screen. In AMPL, this problem is normally solved by keeping the first two indices fixed and defining the values with respect to the third index by means of a list. Regarding the parameter 'a {TIME, MODE, MACH}', which models the machine capacity, this leads to the following assignment (the sign '*' represents the index that is not fixed, which takes the values of the elements of the set 'MACH' in this case):

```
param a
      [1, normal, *]       :=    1    100
                                 2     80
                                 3    110
      [1, overtime, *]     :=    1    120
                                 2     80
                                 3     90
```

```
|2, normal, *|        :=    1     50
                            2     80
                            3    100
|2, overtime, *|      :=    1    110
                            2    100
                            3     80;
```

In mathematical notation, this means that for the first of the two periods of time, $i = 1$ (remember, we have defined TIME := {1, 2} above), the parameter a_{ijh} reads

$$a_{1jk} = \begin{pmatrix} a_{1,normal,1} & a_{1,normal,2} & a_{1,normal,3} \\ a_{1,overtime,1} & a_{1,overtime,2} & a_{1,overtime,3} \end{pmatrix} := \begin{pmatrix} 100 & 80 & 110 \\ 120 & 80 & 90 \end{pmatrix},$$

while we have

$$a_{2jk} = \begin{pmatrix} a_{2,normal,1} & a_{2,normal,2} & a_{2,normal,3} \\ a_{2,overtime,1} & a_{2,overtime,2} & a_{2,overtime,3} \end{pmatrix} := \begin{pmatrix} 50 & 80 & 100 \\ 110 & 100 & 80 \end{pmatrix}$$

for the second period of time, i.e. $i = 2$.

Basically the same approach can be used for parameters with four indices, the parameter 'c {TIME, MODE, PROD, MACH}', for example, which models the production cost. Again, we keep two indices fixed, but as we have two more indices in this case, we have to use a 'double list' in AMPL:

```
param c
         |1, normal, *, *|      :=    1    1    20
                                      1    2    30
                                      1    3    40
                                      2    1    40
                                      2    2    40
                                      2    3    40
                                      3    1    20
                                      3    2    30
                                      3    3    50
         |1, overtime, *, *|    :=    1    1    20
                                      1    2    30
                                      1    3    40
                                      2    1    40
                                      2    2    40
                                      2    3    40
                                      3    1    20
                                      3    2    30
                                      3    3    50
```

```
|2, normal, *, *|      :=    1    1    20
                             1    2    30
                             1    3    40
                             2    1    40
                             2    2    40
                             2    3    40
                             3    1    20
                             3    2    30
                             3    3    50
|2, overtime,*,*|      :=    1    1    20
                             1    2    30
                             1    3    40
                             2    1    40
                             2    2    40
                             2    3    40
                             3    1    20
                             3    2    30
                             3    3    50;
```

In this 'double list', the first row refers to the values of the first index represented by an asterisk (i.e. the elements of the set 'PROD'), the second row refers to the elements of the set 'MACH', and the third row of the list finally assigns the values to our parameter 'c {TIME, MODE, PROD, MACH}'. The definition above implies, for example that

$c_{1,overtime,3,1} = 20$ and $c_{2,normal,1,3} = 40$.

1.3 The complete data file

If we use these methods for all vector parameters for our production problem, add some comments by means of the '#' sign and make sure that we use enough space to write down the data in a well organised, transparent way, we arrive at the following data file.

```
# Data file name:
# C:\Program Files\AmplStudio Modeling System1.6.J\Bin\OR428\ #
ProductionProblemLecture6.dat


################################
### PARAMETERS: SCALARS  ###
################################

# Number of time periods
param T := 2;
# Number of products param
P := 3;
# Number of machines param
M := 3;
```

```
##################################
# #### PARAMETERS: VECTORS
###
##################################
#

# storage capacity {PROD} param
u :=
            1        20
            2        20
            3        0;

# machine capacity {TIME, MODE, MACH}
param a
   [1, normal, *]       := 1     100
                           2     [illegible]
                           3     110

   [1, overtime, *]     := 1     120
                           2      80
                           3      90

   [2, normal, *]       := 1      50
                           2      80
                           3     100

   [2, overtime, *]     := 1     110
                           2     100
                           3      80;

# capacity consumption {TIME, MODE, PROD, MACH}
param t
   [1, normal, *, *] := 1   1   10
                        1   2    8
                        1   3    6
                        2   1    8
                        2   2    6
                        2   3    7
                        3   1   10
                        3   2    5
                        3   3    4

   [1, overtime, *, *]:= 1  1    5
                        1   2    5
                        1   3    5
                        2   1    5
                        2   2    5
                        2   3    5
                        3   1    5
                        3   2    5
                        3   3    5

   [2, normal, *, *] := 1   1    2
                        1   2    3
                        1   3    4
                        2   1    4
                        2   2    4
                        2   3    4
                        3   1    2
                        3   2    3
                        3   3    5
```

```
[2, overtime, *, *]:=  1 1     2
                       1 2     3
                       1 3     4
                       2 1     4
                       2 2     4
                       2 3     4
                       3 1     2
                       3 2     3
                       3 3     5;

# demand {TIME, PROD}
param d :
               1   2   3 :=
             1 25 30  30
             2 30 25  25;

# selling price {TIME, PROD} param
p :
               1       2         3 :=
            1 100 100 90
            2 110 110 100;

# final cheap selling price {PROD} param r
:=
            1         2
            2         2
            3         1;

# storage cost {PROD} param
s :=
            1         1
            2         1
            3         1;

# production cost {TIME, MODE, PROD, MACH} param c
   [1, normal, *, *] := 1   1   20
                        1   2   30
                        1   3   40
                        2   1   40
                        2   2   40
                        2   3   40
                        3   1   20
                        3   2   30
                        3   3   50

  [1, overtime, *, *]:= 1   1   20
                        1   2   30
                        1   3   40
                        2   1   40
                        2   2   40
                        2   3   40
                        3   1   20
                        3   2   30
                        3   3   50
```

```
[2, normal, *, *] := 1  1  20
                     1  2  30
                     1  3  40
                     2  1  40
                     2  2  40
                     2  3  40
                     3  1  20
                     3  2  30
                     3  3  50

[2, overtime, *, *] := 1  1  20
                       1  2  30
                       1  3  40
                       2  1  40
                       2  2  40
                       2  3  40
                       3  1  20
                       3  2  30
                       3  3  50;
```

4. Reading and exercises

<u>Exercise 1</u>
Consider the generalised production plan problem in Exercise 2 of Lecture 6:

a) Set up an AMPL data file for the model data, using the data for Exercise 1 of Lecture 6, use the model file from the exercises of the previous lecture, and solve the problem with AMPLDev. (Please keep the model file for an exercise of a later lecture.)

b) Without using AMPLDev, i.e. just on a sheet of paper, insert the data of Exercise 1 into the general model structure of Exercise 2. Now transform the resulting model instance into its algorithmic representation, i.e. transform the variables and inequalities such that the model instance has the standard form "minimise cx, subject to Ax>=b, x>=0", and determine the matrix A and the vectors b and c that AMPLDev will send to the pre-solver after it has combined the model structure with the model data. (This exercise is just meant to give you a better understanding of what AMPLDev is doing in the background when preparing the model instance for the pre-solver, i.e. what happens after you have created the model and the data files and clicked "solve problem (F9)".)

<u>Exercise 2</u>
Consider Exercise 3 of Lecture 5:

a) Generalise this problem to a Linear Programming problem to the case of T periods of time and j different investment products each of which becomes available for the first time at a certain point of time and is completed after a specific number of periods. The objective is to find an optimal investment portfolio for the entire time horizon, given a certain amount of initial capital at the beginning of period $t = 1$.

b) Programme the model structure with AMPLDev and create a data file that represents with the model data provided at the end of the lecture notes of Lecture 5. Solve the problem with AMPLDev.

Reading:

Required:

- If you have not read it yet: chapter 6 from the AMPLDev User Manual by OptiRisk Systems.

Recommended: ---

Suggested:

- In case you have not done so, Have a look at "AMPL : a modeling language for mathematical programming" by Robert Fourer, David M. Gay, and Brian W. Kernighan (2003), who are the creators of AMPL and read chapters that you think will be helpful.

OR428 – Model Building in Mathematical Programming

Lecture 8: Linear Programming IV
– Analysing the Solution of an LP I: Multiple Optima

Outline:

1. How many optimal solutions does an LP problem have?
2. Recognising multiple optima
3. Reading and exercises

1. How many optimal solutions does an LP problem have?

In the previous lectures we analysed the feasible region of an LP problem and had a look at what characterised the optimal solutions of an LP problem. On this basis, we got an idea of how we can solve an LP problem. Moreover, we had a look at how the professional software packages that are used for solving LP problems (modelling environments) work and have learned the most important concepts of the modelling language AMPL. Now that we can practically solve LP problems and know what happens when solving them, we will have a closer look at the solutions of an LP.

Regarding the optimal solution of an LP there are three options:

1) The LP has exactly one optimal solution, which is an extreme point of the polyhedron that is the feasible region.

2) The LP has no optimal solutions. There are two reasons why this can happen:
   a) The feasible region of the LP is the empty set, i.e. there exists no vector $x \geq 0$ such that $Ax \leq b$. Such an LP is called infeasible.
   b) The feasible region of the LP is unbounded *and* the objection function values increases into the direction where the feasible region is unbounded. Such an LP is called unbounded.

3) The LP has an infinite number of optimal solutions. This is the case when the optimal contour of the objective function coincides with more than just one point of the feasible region, i.e. with a hyperplane that defines the surface of the feasible region. We say the LP has multiple optima.

2. Recognising multiple optima

When we solve a Linear Programming problem, a modelling environment like AMPLDev tells us when the problem is infeasible or unbounded. But if there is an optimal solution, we will not know whether the problem has only one or multiple optima (unless we know so immediately from the way in which our model is built.)

Necessary condition for multiple optima

For an LP to have multiple optima, the objective function must be parallel to a hyperplane that defines the feasible region (in 3-dimesional space this means that the objective function is parallel to a line or a plane on the surface of the polyhedron). An extreme point is optimal if and only if we can derive from the n constraints that define the extreme point a contour of the objective function that represents a valid inequality of the feasible region (i.e. by using non-negative multipliers). Now if the objective function is parallel to one of these constraints or to a combination of them, this means that we do not need all n constraints that define the extreme point to derive the objective function. Consequently, when we have multiple optima, at least one of the multipliers of the n constraints that define the extreme point has the value zero.

In other words: an LP problem has multiple optima **only if** at an optimal extreme point the dual value of an effective constraint is zero, i.e. $y_i = 0$ for some effective constraint $a_{i.}x \leq b_i$, **or** the value of a multiplier of the non-negativity of a non-basic variable is zero, i.e. $ya_{.j} = c_j$ for some non-basic variable x_j.

Sufficient condition for multiple optima

The necessary condition does not guarantee the existence of multiple optima because it can also hold when an optimal extreme point satisfies more than n constraints as equalities. (In this case, more than n constraints happen to intersect at the extreme point in question.) This raises the question of how we can make sure that there really are multiple optima when the necessary condition holds.

A way of doing this is by setting up a new LP problem that is derived from the original LP problem (for which we assume that the optimal solution satisfies the necessary conditions for multiple optimality discussed earlier). Consider the case where we have an LP problem for which the optimal solution is x^* with optimal objective function value $cx^*=\gamma^*$. We may assume with no loss of generality that the LP problem is in maximisation standard form, i.e. all constraints can be written as $Ax\leq b$. Let N denote the index set of all zero valued variables and E the index set of all effective resource constraints, i.e. $N^* = \{j : x_j^* = 0\}$ and $E^* = \left\{i : b_i - \sum_j a_{ij}x_j^* = 0\right\}$.

The new LP problem is now constructed as follows:

1. The resource constraints are the same as in the original LP problem, but we add one more constraint, namely $cx = \gamma^*$. Doing this means that the feasible region of our new problem will consist only of the set of those points that are optimal for the old problem (this feasible set may contain a single element, in which case we have only one unique solution, or it can have more than one element, in which case we have multiple optimal solutions).

2. The objective function of our new LP will be:

$$\max \sum_{j\in N^*} x_j + \sum_{i\in E^*} \left(\left| b_i - \sum_{j} a_{ij} x \right| \right),$$

i.e. the objective is the sum of all zero valued variables and the "slacks" (difference of right hand side minus the value of the left hand side) of the effective constraints at solution x^*.

At the current extreme point, i.e. the solution that we got for the old LP, the value of this new objective function is zero. All other optimal extreme points (if they exist at all) will have a positive value of the objective function (because they are defined by at least one non-negativity and one resource constraint that is different from those that define the current extreme point, and all terms of the two sums are non-negative in any case). In this situation, maximising the value of the objective function means that we try to find any other point of the feasible region that is not the optimal extreme point of the original LP.

If we put these two parts (i.e. the new set of constraints and the new objective function) together, we will have an LP that will look for an extreme point that is an optimal solution of the old LP (because of the new set of constraints) *and* that is not the old optimal solution, if this is possible at all (because of the new objective function). All in all, this means: if our new LP finds an optimal solution that is not the old optimum (or is unbounded), we can be sure that our original LP has multiple optima.

Example:
Consider the following LP problem, for which the optimal solution is x^*=(0, 6.1) with value y^*= 61, and the associated dual vector is y^*= (1, 0, 0, 0, 0).

$$\max\ 2x_1 + 10x_2$$

$$s.t.\ 2x_1 + 10x_2 \leq 61$$

$$2x_1 + 1x_2 \leq 28$$

$$-x_1 + 4x_2 \leq 40$$

$$4x_1 - x_2 \leq 38$$

$$2x_1 + 3x_2 \leq 54$$

$$x_1, x_2 \geq 0$$

We now check whether solution x^* satisfies the necessary conditions for multiple optimality.

Specifically, we check if $y_i = 0$ for some defining resource constraint or

if $\sum y^* a = c$ for some non-basic variable x. The latter condition is satisfied by

the non-basic variable x_1.

Since a necessary condition for multiple optimality is satisfied we proceed with the investigation. To do so we construct and solve new LP problem as follows:

(1) We add the constraint $cx = \gamma^*$, i.e. $2x + 10x = 61$ to the constraints of the original LP problem.

(2) We maximise a new objective function:

$$\sum_{j\in N^*} x_j + \sum_{i\in E^*}\left(b_i - \sum_j a_{ij}x_j\right) = x_1 + b_1 - \sum_j a_{1j}x_j$$

$$= x_1 + 61 - 2x_1 - 10x_2$$

$$= 61 - x_1 - 10x_2.$$

Maximising the new objective function over the augmented set of constraints provides a solution $\bar{x} = (10.5, 4)$, with an optimal objective function value of 10.5.

This means that the original LP problem has multiple optimal solutions and that the new solution is one of the alternative optima. We can verify this is the case by checking that $c\bar{x} = cx^* = 61$ and that the new solution satisfies all the constraints of the original LP problem.

3. Reading and exercises

Exercise 1

Consider the following Linear Programming problem:

minimise $2x_2 - 5x_3$

subject to

$$2x_1 + x_2 + x_3 \le 15$$

$$-2x_1 - 3x_2 + 4x_3 \le -10$$

$$x_1 - x_2 + x_3 \le 9$$

$$x_1, x_2, x_3 \ge 0$$

Solve the problem with AMPLDev. (As this is a very small problem, you do not need separate model and data files.)

a) Identify the basic and non-basic variables, and the effective and ineffective constraints.
b) Does the solution fulfil the necessary condition for multiple optima? If yes, use AMPLDev to find another optimum.
c) Can you give a geometric interpretation of the situation?

Exercise 2

Prove algebraically that the following LP problem is unbounded:

maximise $x_1 + 2x_2$

subject to

$$x_2 \le x_1$$

$$\frac{1}{3}x_1 + 5 \ge x_2$$

$$x_1, x_2 \ge 0$$

(Hint: For doing so, show that there exists a $k \in IR$ such that for every objective function value $\gamma \geq k$ there exists a feasible pair (x_1, x_2) with $x_1 + 2x_2 = \gamma$. Drawing a diagramme of the feasible region might help you .)

Reading:
Suggested: Appa, G (2002): On the uniqueness of solutions to linear programs. In: Journal of the Operational Research Society 53, 1127-1132. (Accessible electronically via the library.)

OR428 – Model Building in Mathematical Programming

Lecture 9: Linear Programming V
– Analysing the Solution of an LP II: Duality

Outline:
1. The primal and the dual LP
2. Interpretation of duality
3. Finding the values related to the solution within AMPLDev
4. Some propositions regarding the primal-dual relationship
5. Reading and exercises

1. The primal and the dual LP problem

In Lecture 8 we have analysed the solutions of LP problems with respect to the number of solutions. We have seen that the number of solutions is related to the values of the dual variables. In the following, we will examine the relationship between the solution of an LP problem and the dual variables in a more general way. We will do so by re-interpreting the optimality conditions that we derived in lecture 4.

These optimality conditions read:

Consider the standard problem

maximise cx

subject to $Ax \square b$
$x \square 0$

with n decision variables and m constraints.

A basic point point x^* is **feasible** (i.e. an extreme point)
if and only if

(F1)	$a_i x^* \square b$	for all **effective** constraints,
(F2)	$a_i x^* \square b$	for all **ineffective** constraints,
(F3)	$x_j^* \square 0$	for all **basic variables**, and
(F4)	$x_j^* \square 0$	for all **non-basic** variables.

The extreme point x^* is **optimal**
if and only if there exists a vector y^* such that

(O1)	$y^* a_j \square c$	for all **basic** variables,
(O2)	$y^* a_j \square c$	for all **non-basic** variables,
(O3)	$y_i^* \square 0$	for all **effective** constraints, and
(O4)	$y_i^* \square 0$	for all **ineffective** resource constraints.

Then the objective function is maximised with $\square^* \square cx^* \square y^* b$. (*)

It is remarkable that there is a great symmetry between the structure of the feasibility conditions (F1) – (F4) and the optimality conditions (O1) – (O4).
In fact, if we swap the roles of basic variables and effective constraints and the roles of non-basic variables and ineffective constraints, the optimality conditions (O1) – (O4) look like the feasibility conditions of a different LP, namely an LP problem with the constraints :

$$A^T y \geq c \qquad y \geq 0$$

(recall that $yA = (A^T y^T)^T$ and that we do not distinguish between row vectors and column vectors if there is no ambiguity). Moreover, because of (*), our new LP problem can be considered to have the objective function

$$yb\,.$$

Finally, we would like to make sense of the feasibility criteria (F1) – (F4) in the light of our new LP problem. If recall the optimality criteria for minimisation problems (Exercise 2, Lecture 4), it is obvious that (F1) – (F4) are the optimality criteria of a *minimisation* problem, namely

$$\min \quad by$$
$$s.t. \quad A^T y \geq c \qquad y \geq 0$$

In sum, we can state:

Primal and Dual LP:

Every LP problem

$$\{\max cx : Ax \square b, x \square 0, x \square IR^n\} \qquad \text{(P)}$$

(the <u>primal problem</u>) is associated with another LP problem

$$\{\min by : A^T y \square c, y \square 0, y \square IR^m\} \qquad \text{(D)}$$

(the <u>dual problem</u>). Finding an optimal solution of the primal problem is equivalent to finding an optimal solution of the dual problem because the optimality criteria of the primal problem are the feasibility criteria of the dual problem, and vice versa.

Regarding the solutions of the primal and the dual, we immediately have the following:

Strong Duality Theorem:

If the primal problem (or the dual problem) is neither infeasible nor unbounded, then both (P) and (D) have an optimal solution. At the point of optimality, the basic variables of the primal problem correspond to the effective constraints of the dual problem, the non-basic variables of the primal problem correspond to the ineffective constraints of the dual problem, and vice versa, and the values of the primal and the dual objective functions are identical.

2. Interpretation of duality

We will now have a look at how we can interpret of the values of the dual problem in view of the original primal problem.

2.1 Interpretation of the dual variables

In Lecture 4, we derived the optimality criteria by expressing a contour of the objective function as a non-negative linear combination of constraints (resource constraints and non-negativities):

$$(yA - w)x = yb$$

$$\Leftrightarrow \qquad cx = \gamma^*$$

This means that the non-negative linear combination of the left hand sides (LHS) of the constraints aimed at 'generating' the coefficients of the objective function from the constraints, i.e.

$$(yA - w)x = cx,$$

while the non-negative linear combination of the right hand sides (RHS) of the constraints results in the value of the objective function, i.e.

$$yb = \gamma^*.$$

From this equation follows a straight-forward interpretation of the values of the dual variables: the dual variables at the point of optimality indicate how much the value of the objective function will increase if the RHS at the corresponding resource constraints is increased by one marginal unit, i.e.

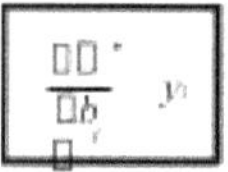

In other words: a (marginal) unit increase in the availability of a resource i (as expressed in the i-th resource constraint) leads to an increase in the objective function value γ^* by the corresponding dual value y of this resource constraint.

Notice that the change in resource constraint can be either up or down. If the constraint is a '≤'-constraint and the problem is maximisation (so at the optimum the dual value is non-negative), then, if the resource increases, so will the objective function, and if the resource decreases, so will the objective function. If a resource constraint is an ineffective constraint, i.e. the dual variable has the value zero, there will be no change in the value of the objective function as the RHS of the constraint changes.

In other words: the dual value of a resource constraint is the marginal value of a resource. Because it reflects the valuation of the resource that is implicit in the production process modelled by an LP, the dual value is also referred to as the shadow price of the resource concerned.

Finally, note that, as it is in general the case with marginal values / derivatives, the marginal value of a resource remains only valid for small increases of the RHS of a constraint, i.e. within a suitably small neighbourhood around the optimum. (Lecture 10 will provide more information about this.)

Example: Consider the LP problem

$$\max 2x_1 + 8x_2$$

$$s.t. \quad \begin{array}{l} x_1 + 3x_2 \le 12 \\ -3x_1 + x_2 \le 0 \end{array}$$

$x_1,\ x_2 \geq 0$ This problem has its optimum at the point $x_1 = 1.2,\ x_2 = 3.6$, at the point of intersection of the two resource constraints, with the dual values of the resource constraints being $y_1 = 2.6,\ y_2 = 0.2$ and an objective function value of $\gamma = 31.2$.

(Prove this as an exercise.) If we increase the RHS of the first resource constraint by 1, i.e. have $b_1 = 13$units of the first resource available, the new optimum is defined by the effective constraints

$$x_1 + 3_2 = 12 + 1 = 13,$$

$$-3x_1 + x_2 = 0$$

which yields $x_1 = 1.3,\ x_2 = 3.9$ and an objective function value of $\gamma = 33.8 = 31.2 + y^1$ (check this as an exercise), i.e. the size and sign of the dual value of the first resource constraints gives the rate of change of the objective function value as the RHS of the first resource constraint changes.

2.2 Interpretation of the dual problem

So far, we have given an interpretation of the value of the dual variables, i.e. the solution of the dual problem. Now let us interpret the dual problem itself. Such an interpretation is not possible in every case, but the following example of a resource allocation problem might serve as an illustration of how a primal maximisation problem is related to a dual minimisation problem.

Let us assume that a factory can produce three types of products, which yield a net profit of c_1, c_2 and c_3 per unit. If we denote the amount of the three products that the factory produces by x_1, x_2 and $x_3 \geq 0$, the owner of the factory is interested in finding a production plan with the objective function

$$\max c_1x_1 + c_2x_2 + c_3x_3.$$

Furthermore, let us assume that the profit the factory can make is restricted by the capacities of machines and storage space. The total machine capacity is given by b_1, while the total storage space is given by b_2. If a_{11}, a_{12}, a_{13} describe the amount of machine capacity that producing one unit of products x_1, x_2, x_3, respectively, requires, and a_{21}, a_{22}, a_{23} describe the amounts of storage space that the production of one unit of these products requires, the owner of the factory is interested in solving the LP

$$
\begin{array}{lll}
\max & c_1 x_1 + c_2 x_2 + c_3 x_3 & \text{(profit)} \\
\text{s. t.} & a_{11} x_1 + a_{12} x_2 + a_{13} x_3 \leq b_1 & \text{(machine capacity)} \\
 & a_{21} x_1 + a_{22} x_2 + a_{23} x_3 \leq b_2 & \text{(storage space)} \\
 & x_1, x_2, x_3 \geq 0 . &
\end{array}
$$

Now let us look at the problem from a different angle. Assume that you are someone who is interested in buying the factory. In this simple case, buying the factory means buying just the machine capacity and the storage space. You do not want to pay too much for the factory, so you try to find out the minimum you have to pay to the factory owner for buying her machines and her storage space. If the variables $y_1, y_2 \geq 0$ denote the amount that you are willing to pay per unit of machine capacity and per unit of storage space, respectively, you are interested in paying

$$\min \quad b_1 y_1 + b_2 y_2 .$$

Of course, you would be happy to pay only one symbolic pound for the factory, but there are some constraints to your offer of buying the factory because you know that the factory owner would agree only when you make a fair offer. In particular, as y_1 is the amount you are willing to pay for one unit of machine capacity and a_{11} is the amount of machine capacity needed for one unit of product 1, $a_{11}y_1$ is the amount you are willing to pay for the machine capacity that is necessary to produce one unit of product 1. Similarly, $a_{21} y_2$ is the amount you are willing to pay for the storage space that is necessary to produce one unit of product 1. Hence, $a_{11} y_1 + a_{21} y_2$ is the entire amount you are willing to pay for being allowed to produce one unit of product 1. Because the factory owner can make a net profit of c_1 by producing and selling one unit of product 1, she will consider your offer fair and agree with it only if

$$a_{11} y_1 + a_{21} y_2 \geq c_1 .$$

Analogous fairness constraints hold for the other two products.

Therefore, in sum, the cheapest *fair* offer for the factory is given by the LP problem

min $\quad b_1 y_1 + b_2 y_2$ (offer for the factory)

s. t.

$a_{11} y_1 + a_{21} y_2 \geq c_1 \; a_{12} y_1 + a_{22}$

$y_2 \geq c_2 \; a_{13} y_1 + a_{23} y_2 \geq c_3 \; y_1 ,$

$y_2 \geq 0 ,$

(fairness constraint w.r.t. prod. 1)
(fairness constraint w.r.t. prod. 2)
(fairness constraint w.r.t. prod. 3)

which is the dual of the problem above.

Within the framework of this interpretation, the Strong Duality Theorem states that the price that you will have to pay for the factory is the same as the profit that the factory owner can make with her factory.

2.3 Interpretation of slack/surplus and reduced cost

There is a third aspect of the dual problem that we should be able to interpret, which is related to those constraints that are not satisfied as equalities.

In the case of a maximisation problem

$$\{\max cx : Ax \leq b, x \geq 0, x \in IR^n\}$$

some resource constraints can happen to be not satisfied as equalities at the point of optimality, i.e.

$$a_i . x^* < b_i$$

for some resource constraints. The difference between the RHS and the LHS, i.e.

$$b_i - a_i x^*$$

is called the slack of the constraint, and it indicates the amount of the resource i that we do not need at the point of optimality.
(Analogously, for a minimisation problem

$$\{\min cx : Ax \geq b, x \geq 0, x \in IR^n\},$$

which might minimise the cost for a production plan provided that a certain minimal output b is achieved, the amount

$$a_i x^* - b_i$$

is called the surplus of constraint i and indicates the amount of output that we do not necessarily need.)

Now every primal maximisation problem

$$\{\max cx : Ax \leq b, x \geq 0, x \in$$

$IR^n\}$ is related to the dual minimisation problem

$$\{\min by : A^T y \leq c, y \geq 0, y \in IR^m\},$$

which, at the point of optimality, might have some resource constraints

$$y^* a. > c$$

that are not satisfied as equalities, i.e. some dual resource constraints might be ineffective and hence have positive surplus variables. This raises the question of how the dual surplus (or dual slack in the case of a standard primal minimisation problem) can be interpreted in terms of the primal problem.

For answering this question we have to recall that at the point of optimality we have

$$y^* a. > c \tag{1}$$

only for the non-basic variables x_j of the primal problem. This means that in the case of a production problem where we maximise the profit we can make with several types of products j, for example, the ineffective dual constraint is related to a product j that is not produced at all at the point of optimality ($x_j = 0$). In contrast to this, all products that we actually produce at the point of optimality have effective dual constraints, i.e.

$$y^* a. = c \tag{2}$$

As a consequence, provided we are interested in producing a product that is currently represented as a non-basic variable in our optimal solution, we would need a situation in which we can make at least so much more profit with this product that the inequality in (1) turns into the equality in (2) (because the optimality conditions demand that a product that we produce, i.e. that corresponds to a basic variable in the primal problem at the point of optimality, corresponds to an effective constraint in the dual problem).

Consequently, $c - y^* a.$

is <u>the amount by which we have to reduce the coefficient c_j in order to make the product so profitable that it becomes part of the optimal production plan</u> (note, in maximisation problems as above, the value of ($c - y^*a.$) is negative so we are in effect increasing the coefficient by ($y^*a. - c$)).

The value $c - y^*a.$ is called the reduced cost of variable x. (The reason for this term is historical and relates better to minimisation problems where the reduced cost of a variable is the amount by which we have to reduce the cost to make the machine, for example, profitable enough to take part in the production process.)

It is possible to give another interpretation of the reduced cost. Assume that you are a factory owner who maximises his profit by using a certain optimal production plan and that a certain product j is not part of that optimal plan. Furthermore, let us assume that producing product j is very important to you (for some other reason) and you would like to produce at least one (marginal) unit of product j. In order to achieve this, you add the additional constraint

$$- x_j \leq -1$$

to the LP problem with which you model your production problem (imagine the '1' in the constraint as a marginal unit). This constraint ensures that the optimal solution will contain the basic variable x_j.

Let us have a look at the dual variable of this resource constraint, which will be satisfied as an equality because it would be even less profitable to produce more than one marginal unit of a product that is not part of the original optimal production plan. If the additional constraint is the k-th constraint, the corresponding dual variable is y_k^*. As this constraint contains only one variable, namely the variable x_j, the optimality condition of the (now) basic variable x_j and the optimality condition of the new constraint are the only optimality conditions that are affected by this new constraint. While the former non-basic variable x_j corresponded to the optimality condition

$y^*a._j > c_j$, the (now) basic variable x_j fulfils the optimality condition

$$y^*a._j - y_k^* = c_j,$$

i.e. the dual variable of the new additional k-th constraint has the value

$$-y_k^* = c_j - y^*a._j,$$

which is the negative value of the reduced cost.
As the dual value of the new effective k-th constraint can be interpreted as the increase of the objective function value that results from changing the constraint

$- x_j \leq -1$ by one marginal unit into the constraint

$$- x_j \leq -1 + 1 = 0,$$

i.e. that results from going back to the original optimal production plan, we can interpret the reduced cost of the (non-basic) variable x_j as the amount by which our profit decreases if we decide to produce one marginal unit of product j.

3. Finding the values related to the solution within AMPLDev

When solving a problem with AMPLDev, you will find most of the relevant data in the output window on the right side of the screen that displays a file called *Solution*.

You will find a table that for every variable with a non-zero value at the point of optimality (i.e. the variable must be a basic variable) provides the value of this variable and its reduced cost (which should be zero for a basic variable, or at least close to zero within the range of tolerance that is necessary due to rounding errors).

Furthermore, AMPLDev can display the *Upper Bound* of each variable. This is due to the option that we can provide AMPL with an additional constraint on the value of the variable. When defining the variable, we can write

var x1 >=0, <= 50;

for example. This definition tells AMPL that there is an additional constraint $x_1 \leq 50$, i.e. an upper bound, on the variable. AMPLDev displays the *U(pper) bound* by typing into the command line:

display NameOfVariable.ub;

The reason for this option is that upper bound constraints can be treated very elegantly within the algorithms that solve LP problems. (You have seen in section 2.3 above that the reduced cost of a lower bound constraint has the same absolute value as its dual value. This relation can be used to streamline an algorithm.) So whenever you know an upper (or lower) bound for a variable, you should write it into the **var**-definition to speed up the algorithm.

You can also find out the reduced costs of a variable if you type

display NameOfVariable.rc;

into the command line at the bottom of the screen.

Regarding the constraints, the constraints table in the *Solution* table shows the slack (or surplus) of the constraints at the point of optimality, the value of the LHS of the constraints (called *Body*), and the dual values of the constraints. If you type in

display NameOfConstraint;

in the command line at the bottom of the screen, AMPLDev will also tell you the dual value of the constraint *NameOfConstraint*.

4. Some propositions regarding the primal-dual relationship

The most powerful theorem regarding the primal-dual relation is the Strong Duality Theorem that was presented in the first section of this lecture. However, there are some other important mathematical statements that are helpful to further clarify the relation between the primal and the dual problem and that are mentioned in the following.

> **Proposition 1**: The dual of the dual is the primal.

This theorem means that if we have a certain primal problem, construct its dual, and then consider the dual problem as a new primal problem from which we construct the dual, we will come back to our original primal problem. In view of the way in which we stated the optimality conditions and the Strong Duality Theorem, this is an obvious result, however it can be proved directly from the definition of dual problem without the optimality conditions (see exercise 3).
A consequence of this proposition is that whenever we have a pair of LP problems that have a primal-dual relationship, it does not matter which of the problems we call the primal problem (and the dual problem). Typically, out of two problems that are dual to each other, a certain problem is called the primal problem when it is in the focus of interest and the modeller has thought of it first.

Another important mathematical statement is the Weak Duality Theorem. While, as the name suggests, the Strong Duality Theorem is the more powerful statement, the Weak Duality Theorem makes an important point in its own right: every feasible solution of a primal maximisation problem has an objective function value that does not exceed the objective function value of any feasible solution of the dual minimisation problem. This property is important in cases where the modeller is interested only in an upper bound of the value of the objective function. Instead of solving the primal problem to optimality, it is sufficient then to find a feasible solution of the dual problem.

> **Proposition 2**: **Weak Duality Theorem**
> If x □ IR^n is a feasible solution of the primal problem
> $$\{\max cx : Ax \, □ \, b, x \, □ \, 0\}$$
> and y □ IR^m a feasible solution of the corresponding dual problem
> $$\{\min by : A^T y \, □ \, c, y \, □ \, 0\},$$
> then
> $$cx \, □ \, \{\max cx : Ax \, □ \, b, x \, □ \, 0\} \, □ \, \{\min by : A^T y \, □ \, c, y \, □ \, 0\} \, □ \, by.$$

Proof: Because of $x \geq 0$ and $A^T y \geq c$, we have

$$cx \leq (A^T y)x = y(Ax),$$

and because of $Ax \leq b$ and $y \geq 0$, it follows

$$cx \leq y(Ax) \leq yb$$

for every feasible solution x of the primal problem and every feasible solution y of the dual problem. This implies

$$cx \le \{\min by : A^T y \ge c, y \ge 0\} \le by$$

for every feasible solution of the primal problem, and

$$cx \le \{\max cx : Ax \le b, x \ge 0) \le by$$

for every feasible solution of the dual problem. Accordingly, we must have

$$\{\max cx : Ax \le b, x \ge 0) \le \{\min by : A^T y \ge c, y \ge 0\},$$

and the entire statement has been proven.

We can now give an overview about the different situations that are possible for a primal-dual pair of LP problems.

Proposition 3: Possibilities of the primal-dual-relationship
For a primal problem

$$\{\max cx : Ax \,\square\, b, x \,\square\, 0)$$

and the corresponding dual problem

$$\{\min by : A^T y \,\square\, c, y \,\square\, 0\},$$

there are four possibilities:

- both problems have a (finite) optimal solution and
  $$\{\max cx : Ax \,\square\, b, x \,\square\, 0) = \{\min by : A^T y \,\square\, c, y \,\square\, 0\},$$
- the primal problem is unbounded and the dual is infeasible,
- the dual problem is unbounded and the primal is infeasible.

both the primal problem and the dual problem are infeasible.

<u>Proof</u>: Possibility (i) follows from the Strong Duality Theorem.
Possibility (ii) follows from the Weak Duality Theorem: if we assume that the primal problem is unbounded, i.e. there exists a $k_0 \in IR$ such that for all $k \ge k_0$ there exists a vector x with $cx \ge k$, <u>and</u> there exists a dual feasible solution, the Weak Duality Theorem yields the contradiction

$$\{\min by : A^T y \ge c, y \ge 0\} \ge k$$

for all $k \ge k_0$. Therefore, the dual problem has no feasible solution.

Possibility (iii) follows from possibility (ii) and the fact that the dual of the dual is the primal.
From a logical point of view, possibility (iv) is the only possibility that remains. Indeed it is possible to have both an infeasible primal and an infeasible dual problem, as the following primal LP problem shows:

$$\begin{aligned} \max \quad & x_1 + x_2 \\ s.t. \quad & \\ & x_1 - x_2 \le -1 \\ & x_2 - x_1 \le -1 \\ & x_1, x_2 \ge 0 \end{aligned}$$

Two more important statements about the primal-dual-relationship are given as (voluntary) exercises 4a) and 4b): Farkas' Lemma and the Complementary Slackness Conditions.

5. Reading and exercises

Exercise 1

A campsite owner, Brown, wants to expand his site, and to persuade a neighbouring small farmer, Smith, to both rent him 30 acres of land and to work for 20 weeks a year for him. Brown wants to determine the prices (rent of land in GBP per acre, and wage in GBP per man-week) he should offer to Smith and which will minimise his total payment.

The constraints which limit Brown's cost minimisation are Smith's opportunities to use the land and his own labour for himself. In other words, the prices of land and labour must be such as to ensure that Smith cannot earn more revenue, by using the land and labour necessary to produce any of the three crops available to him, than by selling them to Brown.

Smith can produce the following crops:

Crop 1 with a net revenue of GBP 7000 per tonne, a land requirement of 10 acres per tonne, and a labour requirement of 3 man-weeks per tonne;
Crop 2 with a net revenue of GBP 5000 per tonne, a land requirement of 6 acres per tonne, and a labour requirement of 2 man-weeks per tonne;
Crop 3 with a net revenue of GBP 3000 per tonne, a land requirement of 2 acres per tonnes, and a labour requirement of 2 man-weeks per tonne.

(a) Formulate Brown's problem as an LP.
(b) Formulate the dual problem to the LP in (a), and consider what meaning you can give to it.
(c) Show that the optimal value of the objective function of the primal problem is equal to the optimal value of the dual problem.

Exercise 2

Consider the Student Exam Problem among the Exercises of Lecture 6 (including the additional exam regulation in part b) .
How many percent could the student improve his grade average when the student's grade is allowed to be 16 marks higher than the lowest paper?

Exercise 3

Prove that the dual problem of the dual problem is the primal problem. (For doing so, restate the dual problem as a maximisation problem and formulate its dual. You do not need more information than just the definition of the dual problem with respect to some primal problem.)

Exercise 4 (Voluntary Exercise)

The following two theorems are very central to the theory of LP duality. You now have the means to prove them.

(*Farkas' Lemma*) Show that either $\{x \in IR^n : Ax \leq b, x \geq 0\} \neq \{\}$ or (exclusive or!) there exists a $z \in IR^m$, $z \geq 0$, such that $zA \geq 0$ and $zb < 0$. (In other words: an LP is either feasible or there exists a hyperplane $\{y : zy = 0\}$ that separates the vector b from the 'cone' of non-negative linear combinations of the columns of A.)

[Hint: consider the LP $\{\max 0x : Ax \leq b, x \geq 0\}$ and its dual, and distinguish between the four different possibilities regarding the solutions of the primal and the dual problem.]

(*Complementary Slackness Conditions*) Let s be the vector of slacks of the primal resource constraints and t the vector of the absolute value of the reduced cost (i.e. the 'slacks' of the dual resource constraints). Prove on the basis of the Strong Duality Theorem that, if x is an optimal solution of the primal problem and y is an optimal solution of the dual problem, then $x_j t_j = 0$ for all j, and $y_i s_i = 0$ for all i.

[Hint: use the definitions of s and t, show that $cx = ub - us - tx$, and draw the conclusion.]

(Note: Our optimality conditions, from where we got the Strong Duality Theorem, already include the Complementary Slackness Theorem. However, the Complementary Slackness Theorem, when proved on the basis of the Strong Duality Theorem as in this exercise, can also be seen as a new proof of our optimality conditions from Lecture 4 – provided the Strong Duality Theorem has been derived from elsewhere, of course. In view of the traditional textbook approach to LP problems, such an alternative way of deriving the Strong Duality Theorem could be an analysis of the Simplex Algorithm.)

Reading:

Required: --

Recommended: chapters 6.1 and 6.2 in Williams (1999).

Suggested: chapters 6.1 to 6.4 in Hillier/Liebermann (2001) on duality theory.

OR428 – Model Building in Mathematical Programming

Lecture 10: Linear Programming VI
– Analysing the Solution of an LP III: Sensitivity Analysis

Outline:
1. Coefficients of the objective function
2. Coefficients of the right-hand side
3. Dual values as marginal values
4. Reading and exercises

1. Coefficients of the objective function

Non-basic variables

Let us start by considering a maximisation problem. If a variable x_j is non-basic, then the optimality condition associated to it is:

(1)

$$\sum y^* a \geq c$$

Clearly then, the coefficient in the objective c_j may decrease to minus infinity without affecting the optimality of the solution. As the coefficient c_j increases there will be a point at which the above condition will be satisfied as an equality and above which the current solution will not be optimal. In a similar fashion we can derive the range for minimisation problems as well.

In general, the ranges for the objective function coefficients of non-basic variables are reported in Table 5 below:

Direction of Objective	Lower limit	Upper limit
maximisation	$-\infty$	$\sum y_i^* a_{ij}$
minimisation	$\sum y_i^* a_{ij}$	$+\infty$

Table 1 Ranges of values for objective function coefficients of non-basic variables

Basic variables

In previous lectures 1 we saw that that for an optimal solution x^*, we can express the objective coefficient of basic variables by combining the rows of coefficient matrix with use of the optimal dual vector y^* as follows:

(2)

$$y^* A^B = c^B,$$

where A^B and c^B contain only the columns corresponding to basic variables.

For the current optimal solution to remain optimal, we must be able to define it by using the same set of constraints and so the basic and non-basic variables will be the same. As a result, if the current solution is to remain optimal, the dual vector should be calculated as in (2) (where one of the coefficients c^B has changed) and should satisfy optimality conditions. In other words, we calculate a range for the objective function coefficient c_j^B by identifying the range of values c_j^B over which the dual vector is calculated as in (2) and yields dual values that satisfy all optimality conditions.

In the 2-dimensional case, varying the coefficient of a basic variable can be interpreted as rotating the objective function as in Figure 1 below. The point x^* remains optimal if the original objective function *Of* is rotated to *Of1* or *Of2* (each parallel one of the constraints of the feasible region), or in fact any objective function 'in-between' these two.

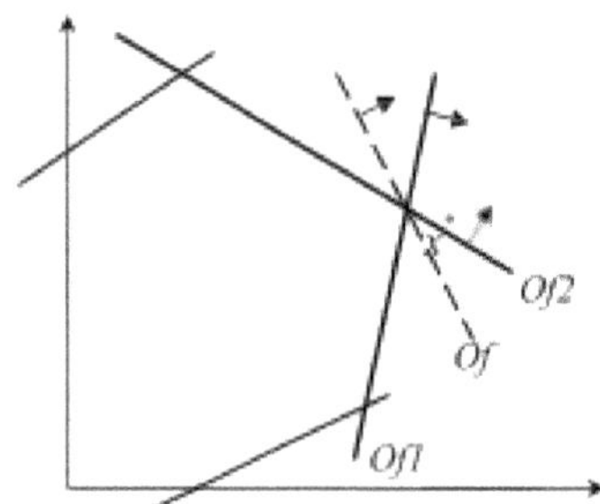

Figure 1 Changing the objective coefficients of a basic variable

Example 3

Consider the following LP problem, for which the optimal solution is $x^*=(1, 0, 2.5, 0)$ and the optimal dual vector is $y^*=(-0.5, 0, 1.5)$.

$$\max\ 7x_1 + 0.5x_2 - 4x_3 - 5x_4$$

$$s.t.\quad x_1 + x_2 + 2x_3 + x_4 \geq 6$$

$$2x_1 + 3x_2 + x_3 - x_4 \leq 5$$

$$5x_1 + x_2 - 2x_3 - 2x_4 \leq 0$$

$$x_1, x_2, x_3, x_4 \geq 0$$

Let us first consider the non-basic variable x_2, for which the optimal condition is:

$$\sum y^* a \geq c.$$

Therefore, c_2 = 0.5 can increase to $\sum y^* a$ = 1 and decrease to $-\infty$ without affecting the optimality condition, i.e. the range for c_2 is $(-\infty, 1]$.

which yields $y_1 = \frac{c_1}{6} - \frac{5}{3}$ and $y_3 = \frac{c_1}{6} + \frac{1}{3}$.

From the optimality conditions we obtain:

$$\text{(a) } y_1 \leq 0 \Rightarrow c_1 \leq 10,$$

$$\text{(b) } y_3 \geq 0 \Rightarrow c_1 \geq -2,$$

$$\text{(c) } \sum_i y_i a_{i2} \geq c_2 \Rightarrow c_1 \geq 5.5,$$

$$\text{(d) } \sum_i y_i a_{i4} \geq c_4 \Rightarrow$$

$c_1 \leq 16$, which gives the overall range $5.5 \leq c_1 \leq 10$.

2 Changing the right hand side of a resource constraint

Effective constraints

Since the dual values can be interpreted as marginal values. we can use the dual values to determine the sensitivity of an LP problem solution to changes in the right hand sides of effective constraints. Notice that the changes in right hand sides can be either positive or negative. If the constraint is a '≤'-constraint and the problem is maximisation (so at the optimum the dual value is non-negative), then, if the resource increases, so will the objective function, and if the resource decreases, so will the objective function. If a resource constraint is an ineffective constraint, i.e. the dual variable has the value zero, there will be no change in the value of the objective function as the right hand side of the constraint changes. The following tables summarise the effects of changes in the right hand sides of resource constraints for both maximisation and minimisation problems:

Constraint	Dual Value	Effect on the objective of:	
		b_i increasing	b_i decreasing
$\leq$	≥ 0 *	increase	decrease
$\geq$	≤ 0 *	decrease	increase
$=$	< 0	decrease	increase
	> 0	increase	decrease
	$= 0$	no change	no change

Table 2. Effects of right hand side changes in maximisation

Constraint	Dual Value	Effect on the objective of:	
		b_i increasing	b_i decreasing
$\leq$	≤ 0 *	decrease	increase
$\geq$	≥ 0 *	increase	decrease
$=$	< 0	decrease	increase
	> 0	increase	decrease
	$= 0$	no change	no change

Table 3. Effects of right hand side changes in minimisation

Note that, as is in general the case with marginal values/derivatives, the marginal value of a resource remains valid only within a given range of changes in the right hand side of a constraint, i.e. within a suitably small neighbourhood around the optimum. This is determined by calculating which range of changes in the right hand have no impact on the definition of the optimal point and the feasibility of the solution (i.e. the range of the right hand side over which the optimal point is defined by the same set of constraints and remains feasible).

Ineffective constraints

If the ineffective constraint is a of sign $\leq$ then clearly the right-hand side can increase to infinity without affecting the solution. The right-hand side can decrease to the value of the left hand side where it is low enough for the constraint to be satisfied as an equality, i.e. decrease to the value below which the current solution would be infeasible. Similarly the right-hand side of a non-defining $\geq$ constraint could decrease to minus infinity and increase to the value of the left hand side, above which the current solution will be infeasible. In general, the ranges for the right hand sides of non-defining constraints are reported in Table 3 below:

Constraint type	Lower limit	Upper limit
$\leq$	$\sum_j a_{ij} x_j^*$	$+\infty$
$\geq$	$-\infty$	$\sum_j a_{ij} x_j^*$

Table 4 Ranges of values for the right hand side of ineffective constraints

Example 2:
Consider the following LP problem, for which the optimal solution is x^*=(10.5, 4) with value 22.5, and the associated dual vector is y^*= (0.31, 0, 0, 0.01, 0).

$$\max x_1 + 3x_2$$

$$s.t.\ 2x_1 + 10x_2 \leq 61$$

$$2x_1 + 1x_2 \leq 28$$

$$-x_1 + 4x_2 \leq 40$$

$$4x_1 - x_2 \leq 38$$

$$2x_1 - 3x_2 \leq 14$$

$$x_1, x_2 \geq 0$$

It can be verified that at the optimal solution is defined by the first and fourth resource constraints. Consider changing the right hand side of the ineffective second resource constraint, i.e. b_2. The value of the left hand side of the constraint at the optimal solution can be calculated to $2\cdot 10.5+3\cdot 4=25$. Therefore, b_2, currently at 28, can decrease to 25 without affecting the feasibility of the solution. Obviously, it can also increase to $+\infty$ without affecting the feasibility of the solution. $b_2 \geq 25$, then the optimality conditions are also not affected. Thus, the range of b_2 over which the current optimal solution remains feasible and, by extension, optimal is $[25,+\infty)$.

Now let us consider the right hand sides of the effective constraints. As discussed above, we can use the dual values to calculate the effect of these changes on the objective function value. Specifically changing the right hand side of any of these two constraints by Δb_i will change the objective by $y_i \cdot \Delta b_i$ (i.e. $0.31 \cdot \Delta b_1$ or $0.01 \cdot \Delta b_4$ respectively).

To see why the dual values remain valid over a limited range for b_i consider the range for $b_1 = [40, 82]$. If we change the current value of b_1 to any value within this range, the same constraints define the optimal solution. In other words, feasibility is unaffected and so the dual values remain unchanged and can be seen to satisfy the optimality conditions. The following figure illustrates this point.

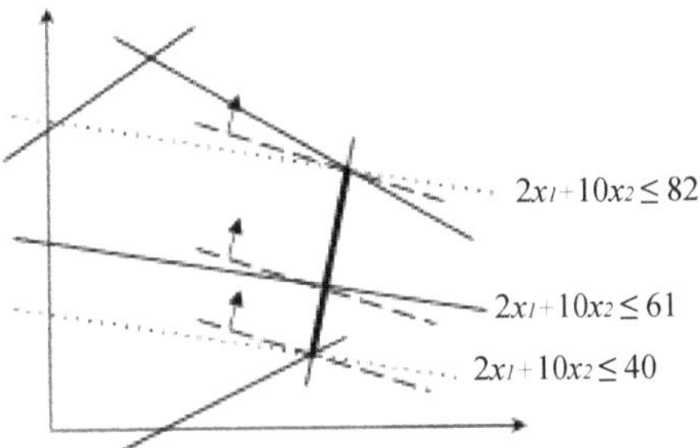

Figure 2. Sensitivity analysis range for the right hand side of b_1

We now consider how we may calculate the range for b_1 over which the interpretation of the dual values remains valid. For this set of dual values to have a meaning, we must ensure that the same constraints are used to define the optimal point over the entire range for b_1. So in this example we must ensure that for any value of b_1 the following two equations are collectively satisfied:

$$2x_1 + 10x_2 = b_1$$

$$4x_1 - x_2 = 38$$

Solving these gives $x_1 = \dfrac{b_1 + 380}{42}$ and $x_2 = \dfrac{2b_1 - 38}{21}$. For this point to remain optimal it must be feasible, i.e. it must satisfy the remaining constraints of the LP. Using these inequalities we can identify bounds for b_1 as follows:

$$\text{(a) } x_1 \geq 0 \Rightarrow \frac{b_1 + 380}{42} \geq 0 \Rightarrow b_1 \geq -380$$

$$\text{(b) } x_2 \geq 0 \Rightarrow \frac{b_1 + 380}{42} \geq 0 \Rightarrow b_1 \geq 17,$$

$$\text{(c) } 2x_1 + 1x_2 \leq 28 \Rightarrow b_1 \leq 82,$$

$$\text{(d) } -x_1 + 4x_2 \leq 40 \Rightarrow b_1 \leq 157.6,$$

$$\text{(e) } 2x_1 + 3x_2 \leq 14 \Rightarrow b_1 \geq 40,$$

which we may combine to give the overall range $40 \leq b_1 \leq 82$.

Finally, we investigate the changes to the objective when the value of b_1 varies beyond the above limits. Inevitably this involves having to resolve the LP problem for a pre-determined set of possible values for b_1. In Figure 3, below, the bold line segments indicate the locus of optimal solutions for values of b_1 between 10 and 150. Note that at each extreme point at which the definition of the optimal point changes, there are two different dual solutions (one of these corresponds to the definition of the optimal point which involves the constraint under investigation), which then remain constant within the range of b_1 over which the solution remains feasible. The sequence of solutions and associated dual vectors is reported in Table 4. The two plots in Figure 4 illustrate how the value of the objective as well as the dual value y_1 vary with the value of b_1. Notice that the plot of the dual values is a step function.

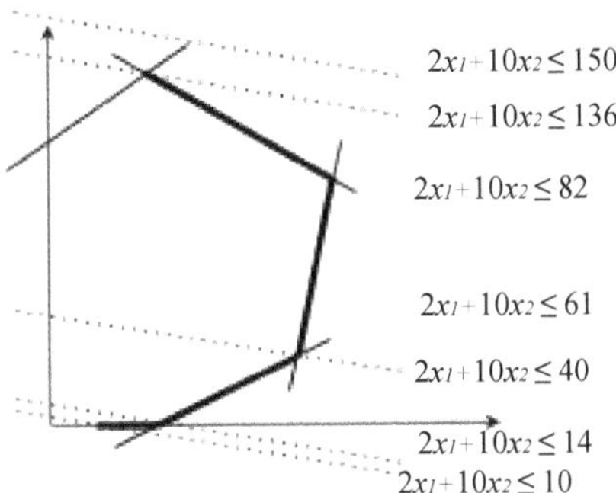

Figure 3. Investigating extensive changes in b_1

b_1	x_1	x_2	y_1	y_2	y_3	y_4	y_5	Objective
10	5	0						5
			0.5	0	0	0	0	
14	7	0						7
			0.346	0	0	0	0.154	
40	10	2						16
			0.31	0	0	0.095	0	
82	11	6						29
			0.278	0.222	0	0	0	
136	8	12						44
			0	0.778	0.556	0	0	
150	8	12						44

Table 5 Optimal solutions and associated dual vectors for different values of b_1

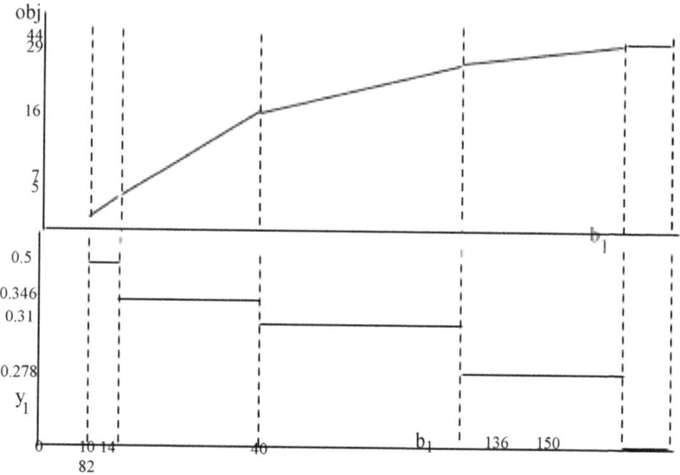

Figure 4 Objective function value and dual value y_1 plotted against the value of b_1

3. Reading and exercises

<u>Exercise 1</u>

Analyse the solution of the Fleet Enlargement Problem (week 1) and answer the following questions:

(a) Within which range can the maintenance capacity change without affecting the optimal solution?

(b) If the company were interested in buying more planes: how much should they pay for additional pilots? Which is the interval of the number of pilots for which this answer remains valid?

(c) The company's strategy should be flexible enough such that they will be able to deal with new competitors that enter the market, which might include a situation of decreasing fare levels in the next years. Within which interval of annual net profits per plane would the enlargement plan remain optimal?

(d) Under which circumstances would it be reasonable for the Board of Directors to increase the budget for the fleet enlargement project? Which is the interval of the budget for which this answer remains valid?

(e) Assume that the company finances the new planes on the basis of (constant) capital cost of 6% per year. Which price would the manufacturer of the medium range plane have to offer to make their product profitable for the airline?

Exercise 2

This lecture has analysed the sensitivity of the model parameters b and c. Using the same approach that has been used in this lecture, i.e. by examining the consequences of parameter changes for the feasibility and optimality conditions, it is possible to analyse the sensitivity of a model instance with respect to changes of the A-matrix. Analogously to what has been done in this lecture, derive general formulations of the conditions under which a basic point of a Linear Programming problem remains feasible or optimal with respect to the same effective constraints and the same non-basic variables

(a) when you change a coefficient of the A-matrix in the row of an ineffective constraint and the column of a non-basic variable,

(b) when you change a coefficient of the A-matrix in the row of an effective constraint and the column of a non-basic variable,

(c) when you change a coefficient of the A-matrix in the row of an ineffective constraint and the column of a basic variable.

(The fourth case, i.e. the case in which you change a coefficient in the row of an effective constraint and the column of a basic variable, is beyond our scope.)

Reading:

Required: --

Recommended: chapters 6.3 to 6.5 in Williams (1999).

Suggested:

(a) Chapters 6.5 to 6.8 in Hillier/Liebermann (2000) on sensitivity analysis
(b) Chapter 5 of Bertsimas/Tsitsiklis on sensitivity analysis (this chapter gives a more theoretical treatment that goes beyond the scope of this lecture).

OR428 – Model Building in Mathematical Programming

Lecture 11: Integer Programming I – Basic Concepts, Branch-&-Bound

Outline:
1. PIP, MIP and BIP problems
2. The feasible region of a PIP problem
3. Typical problems that lead to an IP approach
4. LP relaxation and rounding as a method for solving an IP?
5. The standard algorithm: Branch-&-Bound
6. Reading and exercises

1. PIP, MIP and BIP problems

The Linear Programming problems that we have analysed in the previous lectures had one aspect in common: the variables were continuous values, i.e. they could be rational numbers within certain intervals (given by the feasible region). In many practical problems, however, we require discrete values for at least some variables. Recall the fleet enlargement problem among the exercises of Lecture 1, for example. When we solved the problem, we simply ignored the fact that planes come in integer numbers as there are no half or quarter planes. So what we need to solve such a problem properly, is a way of making sure that the number of planes the model calculates is integer.

Let us start with some definitions.

Integer Programme (PIP):

$cx \; Ax \leq b \; x \geq 0,$

$x \in Z^n$

Binary Integer Programme (BIP):

$cx \; Ax \leq b \; x \geq 0,$

$x \in \{0,1\}^n$

Mixed Integer Programme (MIP):

max c_1

$s.t$ x_1

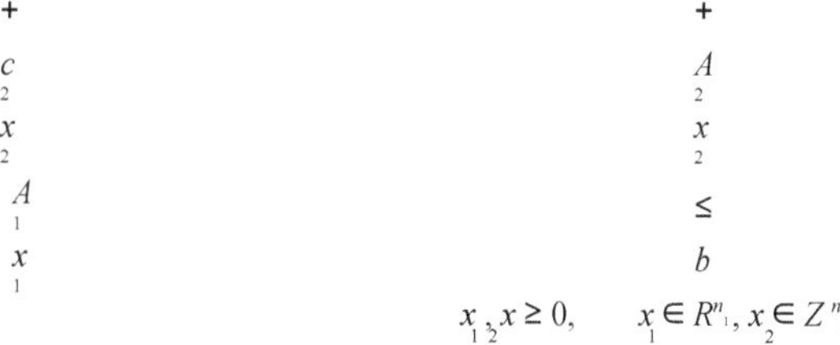

$$x_1, x_2 \geq 0, \qquad x_1 \in R^{n_1}, x_2 \in Z^{n_2}$$

We will use the term Integer Programme (IP) to refer to either of these problems. For solving them with AMPL, you just have to add the word 'integer' in the variable definition, e.g.: `var PlanesHired{Time,Planes} integer >=0;`

2. The feasible region of a PIP

Consider the following PIP problem:

$$\max z = 2x_1 + 5x_2$$

$$s.t. \quad 12x_1 + 5x_2 \leq 60$$

$$2x_1 + 10x_2 \leq$$

$$35$$

$$x_1, x_2 \geq 0 \text{ and Integer}$$

The feasible region is illustrated in Figure 1 below, where the dots are the feasible integer points.

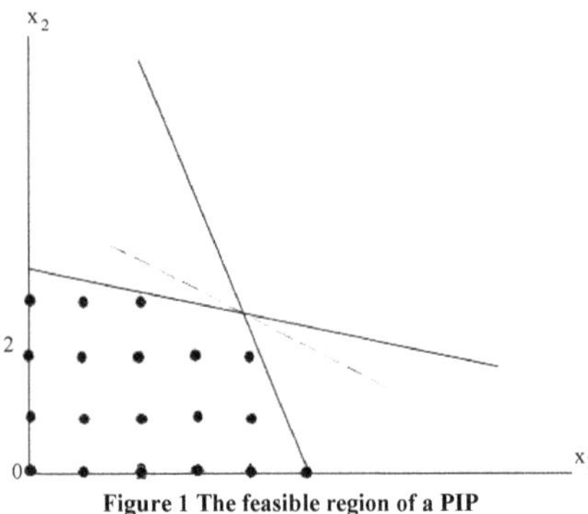

Figure 1 The feasible region of a PIP

The linear program optimum is at the point $x_1 = 3.864$, $x_2 = 2.727$ and the objective function $z = 2x_1 + 5x_2$ is 21.364. Visually we can see that the possible optimum points are ($x_1 = 2$, $x_2 = 3$) with $z = 19$, and ($x_1 = 4$, $x_2 = 2$) with $z = 18$.

This diagram shows the optimum solution is not necessarily an extreme point, in general, it will *not* be an extreme point. LP problems are easy to solve because we know that at least one of optimal points will be an extreme point. This wonderful property is completely lost in the case of integer programs.

3. Typical problems that lead to an IP approach

Many practical problems can be solved by an IP approach. For practical purposes, we can distinguish the following cases:

1. The fleet enlargement problem belongs to a class of problems for which an IP approach is helpful because the problem is about determining optimal discrete activities (i.e. buying a discrete number of planes).

2. A problem that belongs to a related class would be a production problem in which we have to determine the number of machines that we use for carrying out a specific production schedule. Such a problem would be about finding an optimal way

of using discrete resources.

3. In many cases, cost functions do not only include variable cost, but also fixed cost, cost for setting up a new factory, for example. Problems of this type have a non- continuous objective function, namely an objective function that has the value zero when the factory, for example, is not used and that has a value that equals some fixed cost plus some variable cost when the factory is used (the variable cost would be the production cost per unit, while the fixed cost are incurred by setting up the factory in the first instance).

4. Many practical problems contain logical conditions. An example would be a problem in which a certain machine can be used only when we have used a particular other machine before. Logical conditions of this type can be modelled with an IP in a very direct way.

5. Some problems come with a non-linear objective function or a non-convex feasible region. In these cases, the problem can often be approximated by linear and convex sub-problems, which are 'connected' via integer variables.

6. Another very common type of problems where an IP approach makes sense is the class of combinatorial problems. Roughly speaking, combinatorial problems arise when we have a set of discrete items and would like to find an optimal subset of it. Many problems that be represented by graphs, for example, belong to this class of problems.

4. LP relaxation and rounding as a method for solving an IP?

The difference between a Linear Programming problem and an IP problem consists in the fact that the IP has additional constraints, namely the integrality constraints. A problem B that is derived from a problem A by not taking into account some of the latter's constraints is called a relaxation of this problem. When we disregard the integrality constraints of an IP problem, we arrive at a normal LP problem. Therefore, such an LP problem is called the LP relaxation of an IP problem. As the LP relaxation has a larger feasible region than the original IP, the objective function value of an IP can never be better as the LP relaxation of the problem. In other words: For a maximisation problem, the LP relaxation of an IP problem provides an upper bound of the objective function value of the optimal solution of the IP problem.

Under which circumstances does it make sense to solve the LP relaxation of an IP problem and round the solution?

1. The rounded solution is feasible, AND
2. The difference between the upper bound of the objective function value that the LP relaxation provides and the objective function value of the rounded feasible solution is acceptable for the practical purpose that the model serves.

5. The standard algorithm: Branch-&-Bound

A lot of research has been and is being applied to methods to solve integer programming problems. One of the most successful approaches to date is *branch and bound.* All the commercial mathematical programming systems offer an integer programming solution procedure based on some variation of branch and bound.

Branch and bound can be thought of as a systematic exploration of the feasible region and an elimination of those parts which can be shown either not to contain an integer solution or not to contain the optimal solution.

The principle of the branch and bound algorithm is that the feasible region is partitioned into a collection of smaller regions. Each region is itself represented by linear constraints and the objective function can be optimised over these smaller regions. The partitions of the feasible region can themselves be further partitioned into even smaller regions. An upper bound on the value of the objective function, for a partition and all its sub-partitions, is the optimal value of the objective function over the feasible region defined by the partition. In practice, the partitioning of the feasible region is performed sequentially - that is the branching operation. The bounding operation determines the choice of partition on which to perform the branching operation. The algorithm is best represented by a tree graph.

An example of the branch and bound algorithm

Let us return to the example we considered earlier. The algorithm starts by solving the problem as an LP. This corresponds to the *root node* of the *branch and bound tree*. If the solution satisfies the integer condition stop, otherwise it is necessary to branch. Select a variable whose value is non-integer and create two new sub- problems. The constraints of the new sub-problems are so chosen that the current non- integer solution is feasible in neither sub-problem.

In the example, the solution at the root node is: $x_1 = 3.864$, $x_2 = 2.727$. We arbitrarily choose to branch on x_1. This is done by creating two sub-problems: one with the extra constraint $x_1 \leq 3$ and the other with $x_1 \geq 4$.

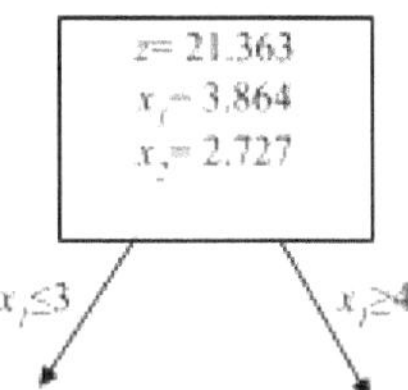

We choose (arbitrarily) to solve the 'left-hand' problem first. This gives a solution of $z = 20.5$, $x_1 = 3$ and $x_2 = 2.9$. Notice that because an additional constraint, $x_1 \leq 3$, has been added, the value of the objective function, z, either stays the same or decreases. As x_2 is non-integer two further sub-problems with the constraints $x_2 \leq 2$ and $x_2 \geq 3$ are created. There are now three unsolved sub-problems.

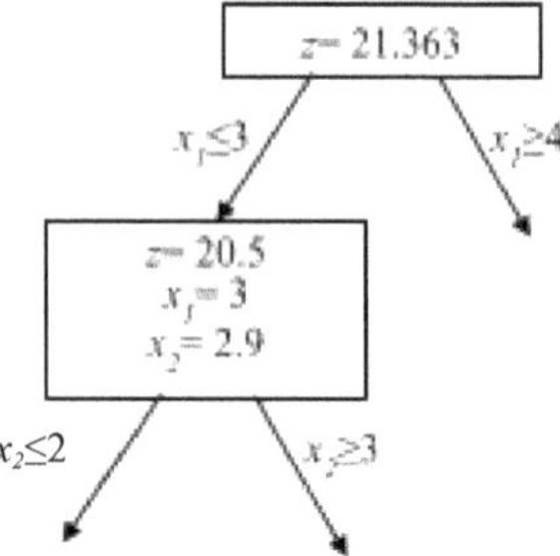

If we now solve the leftmost problem again this gives an integer solution $z = 16$, $x_1 = 3$, $x_2 = 2$. This solution becomes *incumbent solution*, i.e. the best known so far. The branch is said to be *fathomed by integrality* and now the algorithm *backtracks* and selects one of the unsolved sub-problems for solution. Arbitrarily choosing the most recently formed unsolved sub-problem and solving it gives the tree below.

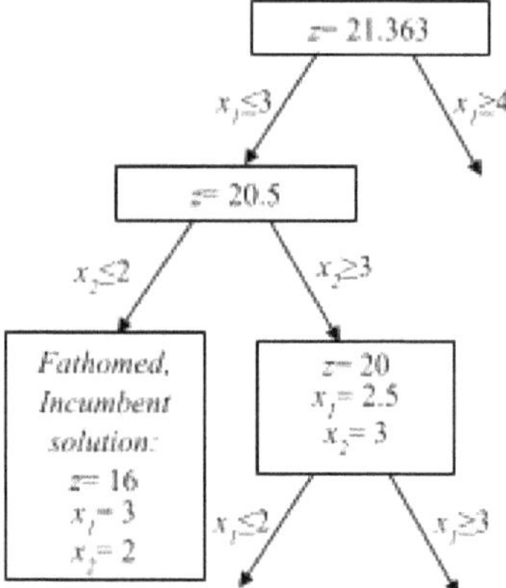

Continuing branching and solving gives the tree below. A better integer solution of $z = 19$, $x_1 = 2$, $x_2 = 3$ is found and becomes the new incumbent. A branch is *fathomed by infeasibility*, and so backtracking occurs, if a sub-problem is infeasible.

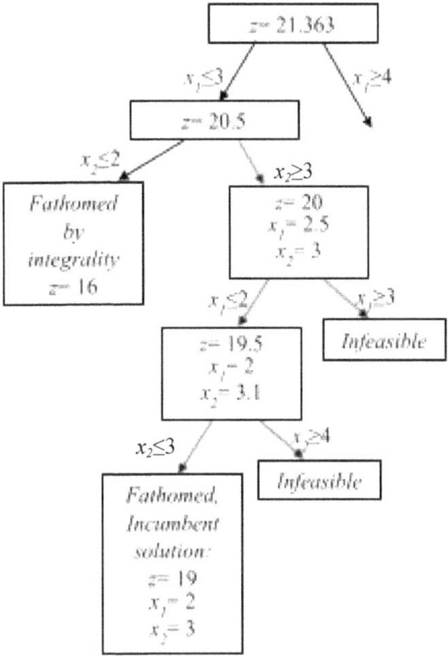

At this point the entire branch of the tree where $x_1 \leq 3$ is completely fathomed. So we backtrack to the very beginning and solving the sub-problem with the single extra constraint $x_1 \geq 4$. Continuing in the same fashion as before gives the tree below and subsequently branching gives the tree below.

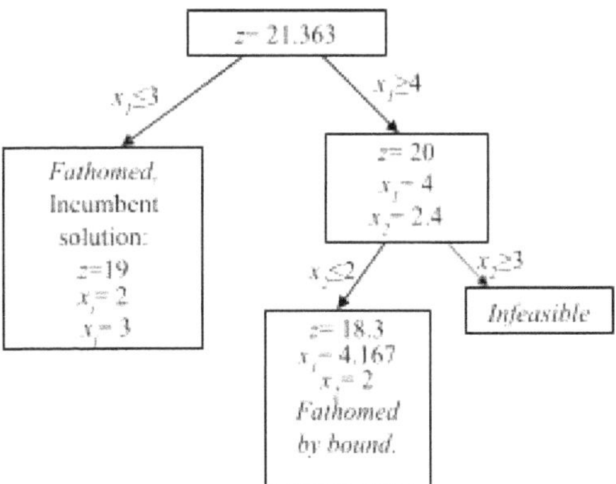

As extra constraints are added to form the sub-problems, the value of the objective function cannot increase, it either stays the same of decreases. At the sub-problem with z = 18.3 the maximum objective function value that can be found by further branching on this sub-problem is less than or equal to 18.3. However we have a better solution at z = 19 so because of the bound there is no point in continuing to branch. Thus the sub-problem with z = 18.3 is *fathomed by bound.*

The incumbent, and thus optimal solution to the problem at the end of the branch and bound search is $x_1 = 2$, $x_2 = 3$ with an objective function value of 19.

Notice that in order to solve this problem in 2 variables it was necessary to solve 11 linear programs. This is true in general, it requires substantially more work to solve an integer program than a linear program. That is why great care should be taken in setting up an integer program - do the variables really have to take integer values?

6. Reading and exercises:

Exercise 1

Consider the following IP:

$$\max \quad x_1 + 0.64x_2$$

$$s.t. \quad \begin{aligned} 50x_1 + 31x_2 &\leq 250 \\ 3x_1 - 2x_2 &\geq -4 \\ x_1, x_2 &\geq 0 \\ x_1, x_2 &\in N \end{aligned}$$

a) Solve the LP relaxation of the model with AMPLDev. If you round the solution, is it feasible?

b) Solve the IP problem by performing a Branch-&-Bound search MANUALLY, i.e. add appropriate constraints to the LP relaxation and solve the resulting LP problems with AMPLDev until your tree search has made you find the optimum.

Exercise 2

An engineering factory makes 7 products (PROD1 to PROD7) on the following machines:

4 Grinders
2 Vertical drills
3 Horizontal drills
1 Borer
1 Planer

Each product yields a certain contribution to profit (defined as £/unit selling price minus cost of raw materials). These quantities (in £/unit) together with the unit production times (hours) required on each process are given below. A dot indicates that a product does not require a process.

	PRODUCT						
	1	2	3	4	5	6	7
Contribution to profit	10	6	8	4	11	9	3
Grinding	0.5	0.7	.	.	0.3	0.2	0.5
Vertical drilling	0.1	0.2	.	0.3		0.6	.
Horizontal drilling	0.2	.	0.8	.	.	.	0.6
Boring	0.05	0.03	.	0.07	0.1	.	0.08
Planing	.	.	0.01	.	0.05	.	0.05

Each machine must be down for maintenance in one month of the six apart from the grinding machines only two of which need to be down in any one of the six months.

There are marketing limitations on each product in each month. These are:

	PRODUCT						
	1	2	3	4	5	6	7
January	500	500	0	500	1000	500	100
February	1000	200	0	200	300	60	500
March	300	0	500	0	0	0	500
April	300	400	400	100	200	100	100
May	800	300	100	300	300	500	300
June	200	150	600	600	400	100	1000

It is possible to store up to 100 of each product at a time at a cost of £0.5 per unit per month. There are no stocks at present but it is desired to have a stock of 50 of each type of product at the end of June.

The factory works a 6 day week with 2 shifts of 8 hours each day. It may be assumed that each month consists of only 24 working days.

When and what should the factory make in order to maximize the total profit? (No sequencing problems need be considered.)

Reading:

Required: --
Recommended: Williams: Chapter 8,
Hillier/Liebermann: Chapters 12.1, 12.2 and 12.5-7.

Suggested: Bertsimas/Tsitsiklis: Chapter 11 for alternative solution methods

OR428 – Model Building in Mathematical Programming

Lecture 12: Integer Programming II – Modelling Techniques I

Outline:

In the previous lecture we have introduced the concept of Integer Programmes. This lecture and the following Lecture 15 are intended to give you an overview of the most important modelling techniques for Integer Programmes and illustrate that the integrality constraints that turn an LP problem into an IP problem provide us with a powerful mathematical structure that allows us to model problems that are beyond reach within the framework of Linear Programming problems (albeit at the price of much longer computation times).

1. Indicator variables

Indicator variables are binary (0/1) variables that take their values depending on whether or not a certain condition holds. In the following, δ will denote an indicator variable. We consider two cases:

1.1 Indicator variables for '$x > 0$'

A common situation is a problem that includes the relationship

$$(x > 0) \rightarrow (\delta = 1)$$

This relationship can be modelled by the constraint

$$x \leq M\delta$$

where M is a constant coefficient that is large enough to be a valid upper bound for x (note that it is advisable to choose the smallest bound possible in order to reduce computational time)

Example:

A typical practical application of this would be the case where we have fixed cost once we produce a certain product. For modelling this, we need the constraint above and the expression

$$c_1 x + c_2 \delta$$

in the objective function. If no production takes place then $x=0$ and so also $\delta=0$ in which case no cost is incurred. On the other hand, if some product is produced then $x>0$ which will imply that $\delta=1$ so that we will incur the fixed cost c_2 but also the appropriate variable cost $c_1 x$.

Another important case is the converse relationship

$$(\delta = 1) \rightarrow (x > 0)$$

To model this relationship, we have to define a minimal threshold m such that $\delta = 1$ implies $x > m$ (i.e. any value of x less than m is considered equivalent to 0). That is we will instead model the relationship

$$(\delta = 1) \rightarrow (x \geq m) .$$

This can be done by enforcing the constraint

$$x \geq m\delta .$$

The above two methods are known as the *big-M method* and the *small-m method.*

1.2 Indicator variables for valid constraints

As a generalisation of the ideas above, it is also possible to use indicator variables to show whether a certain constraint holds. If we would like to model the relationship

$$(\delta = 1) \rightarrow (ax \leq b) ,$$

(or equivalently $(ax > b) \rightarrow (\delta = 0)$)

we can do so by using the constraint

$$ax - b \leq M(1 - \delta) ,$$

with M being a valid upper bound for the expression $ax - b$.

For modelling the converse relationship

$$(ax \leq b) \rightarrow (\delta = 1) ,$$

we will use a threshold ε that corresponds to the value of $(ax - b)$ beyond which we consider the constraint violated, and will instead model the relationship

$$(\delta = 0) \rightarrow (ax \geq b + \varepsilon).$$

This can be done by means of the constraint

$$ax - b \geq (1-\delta)\varepsilon + m\delta ,$$

with m being an appropriate lower bound for $ax - b$.

Analogous expressions with indicator variables can be built for the constraint $ax \geq b$. The statement

$$(\delta = 1) \rightarrow (ax \geq b)$$

$$\text{(or equivalently } (ax < b) \rightarrow (\delta = 0))$$

can be expressed by

$$ax - b \geq m(1-\delta) ,$$

while the converse statement

$$(ax \geq b) \rightarrow (\delta = 1)$$

is modelled indirectly (as before) by using the threshold ε and considering the relationship

$$(\delta = 0) \rightarrow (ax \leq b - \varepsilon) ,$$

which can be modelled by means of the constraint

$$ax - b \leq (\delta - 1)\varepsilon + M\delta .$$

The modelling techniques presented here can be combined to model more complex statements. This can be done, for example, by using two indicator variables each of which is used to model one of the statements above and introducing a third indicator variable to express a logical condition (such as: if the third indicator variable is zero, at least one of the other two indicator variables must be zero, too).

2. Logical conditions

Binary variables, i.e. integer variables with the upper bound of 1, allow us to model logical conditions, i.e. constraints expressed in terms of 'and', 'or', 'not', 'if ... then', 'only if ... then', 'if and only if ... then', 'either ... or'.

Typical practical problems where this type of constraints is necessary are (taken from Williams (1999)):

- If no depot is sited here then it will not be possible to supply any of the customers from this depot.
- If the library's subscription to this journal is cancelled then we must retain at least one subscription to another journal in this class.

- If we manufacture product A, we must also manufacture product B or at least one of the products C and D.

- If this station is closed then both branch lines terminating at the station must also be closed.
- No more than five of the ingredients in this class may be included in the blend at any one time.
- If we do not place an electronic module in this position then no wires can connect into this position.
- Either operation A must be finished before operation B starts or vice versa.

Let us assume we have two expressions X1 and X2 that are to be related via logical conditions. For doing so, we introduce indicator variables x1 and x2 that are one when X1 and X2 are true, respectively, and zero otherwise. Now we can add the following constraints:

$x1 + x2 \geq 1$	for 'X1 or X2',
$x1 = 1,\ x2 = 1$	for 'X1 and X2',
$x1 = x2$	for 'X1 $\leftrightarrow$ X2',
$x1 = 1 - x2$	for 'X1 $\leftrightarrow$ not X2',
$x1 \leq x2$	for 'X1 $\rightarrow$ X2',
$x1 + x2 = 1$	for 'either X1 or X2'.

Remarks:

1. This concept can be generalised to longer, more complicated expressions of more than two expressions.
2. Logical conditions often can be transformed into other logical expressions. "not (X1 and X2)", for example, is equivalent to "(not X1) or (not X2)". Similarly, "X1 $\rightarrow$ X2" is equivalent to "(not X1) or X2".
3. The constraints for the condition 'X1 and X2' have been mentioned here because they can be used when an 'and'-condition is part of a larger, more complex logical expression. In the case of a simple 'and'-statement we do not need indicator variables. It is part of the concept of LP and IP problems that every constraint establishes an 'and'-relationship with the other constraints. This implies that for an expression like 'X1 and X2' it is normally sufficient just to add the expressions X1 and X2 as regular constraints.

Example: Let us assume we have to model
'(X1 or X2) $\rightarrow$ (X3 or X4 or X5)'.

We introduce indicator variables x_1 to x_5 corresponding to the expressions X1 to X5 in the way described above, and keep in mind that the relationships 'X1 or X2' and 'X3 or X4 or X5' can be modelled by means of the constraints:

$$x_1 + x_2 \geq 1$$

$$x_3 + x_4 + x_5 \geq 1$$

What we have to do now is to model the statements

$$(x_1 + x_2 \geq 1) \rightarrow (\delta = 1)$$

$$(\delta = 1) \rightarrow (x_3 + x_4 + x_5 \geq 1)\ .$$

This can be achieved by using the constraints given in the previous sub-section about indicator variables.

Using the appropriate values: $M = 1, m = -1, \varepsilon = 1$

we model the above relationship by the following two statements:

$$x_1 + x_2 \leq 2\delta$$

$$x + x + x \geq \delta .$$

3. Discrete values for a variable or the RHS of a constraint

In some practical applications it is necessary to restrict the value of a variable to a discrete set of values $\{b_1, b_2, \ldots, b_m\}$. Such a case could be a company where the production level can only take discrete values, for example. This situation can be modelled by the constraints

$$x \; \sum_{i=1}^{m} b_i \delta_i$$

$$\sum_{i=1}^{m} \delta_i$$

using binary variables $\delta_i \in \{0,1\}, i = 1,\ldots, m$. The second constraint ensures that

exactly one of the variables δ_i is one, while the others are zero (if necessary we can introduce different cost coefficients for these distinct values in the objective function by adding to the objective function the term:

$$\sum_{i=1}^{m}$$

The same idea can also be used for restricting the RHS of a constraint to a discrete set of values. This is done again by using binary variables $\delta_i \in \{0,1\}, i = 1,\ldots, m$ introducing the constraints:

and

$$\sum_{j=1}^{n} a_j x_j \leq \sum_{i=1}^{m} b_i \delta_i$$

$$\sum_{i=1}^{m} \delta_i \; 1$$

A practical application of this would be a machine that can be used only for a discrete set of capacities, or a problem with different levels of investment that extend the capacity of a production plant.

4. Piecewise linear objective functions

In practical problems, objective functions are not always entirely linear. We could have, for example, a maximisation problem with increasing returns to scale. This can happen, for example, when a higher number of goods produced leads to lower variable cost per unit of the product. In the following, we will consider a continuous objective function that is piecewise linear in one variable (the idea used here can be generalised to objective functions that are piecewise linear in more than one variable and to objective functions that are piecewise linear, but not continuous).

The function we will consider can be imagined as follows:

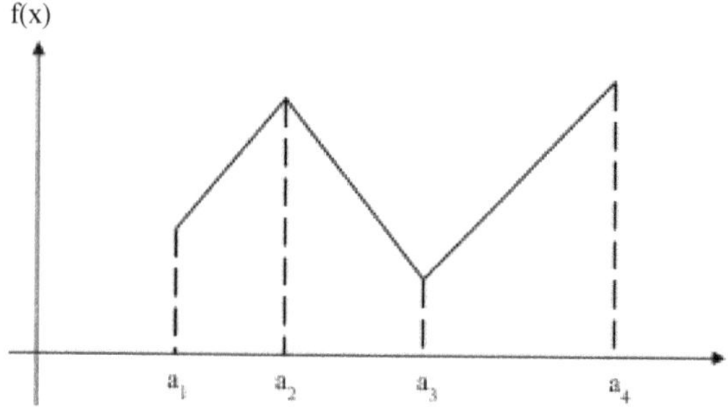

This means we have a set of points $(a_i, f(a_i))$ for $i = 1, 2, ..., k$ that define a continuous piecewise linear function on the interval $[a_1, a_k]$. The points $(a_i, f(a_i))$ can be imagined as points on he graph of a non-linear function which we wish to approximate by a collection of piecewise linear segments as above.

Note that for any $x \in [a_i, a_{i+1}]$ we can express x, by using non-negative variables θ_i and θ_{i+1}, as a convex combination of a_i and a_{i+1}:

$$x = \theta_i a_i + \theta_{i+1} a_{i+1} \quad \text{and} \quad \theta_i + \theta_{i+1} = 1.$$

Using these values of θ_i and θ_{i+1} we can approximate the true value of $f(x)$ by combining $f(a_i)$ and $f(a_{i+1})$ as follows

$$f(x) = \theta_i f(a_i) + \theta_{i+1} f(a_{i+1}).$$

So, to approximate the value of $f(x)$ for any $x \in [a_1, a_k]$ we could use continuous variables $\theta_i \in \{0,1\}$, $i = 1,..., k$ and the constraints:

$$x = \sum_{i=1}^{k} \theta_i a_i$$

$$f(x) = \sum_{i=1}^{k} \theta_i f(a_i)$$

$$\sum_{i=1}^{k} \theta_i = 1,$$

provided we can also enforce the *additional* restriction that only two consecutive variables θ_i can be positive and all other θ_i equal to zero.

We do this introducing binary variables $\delta_i \in \{0,1\}$, $i = 1,\ldots, k-1$ which we will use to represent if a point x is in one of the intervals $[a_i, a_{i+1}]$ or not, i.e. a binary variable has the value one if and only if the variable x is within the corresponding interval (if x is on the boundary of two intervals, our IP will choose arbitrarily one interval).

Then, if we would like to maximise the function f, we can set up the following IP problem (further constraints and variables can be added according to the practical problem at hand):

$$
\begin{aligned}
\text{maximise} \quad & \sum_{i=1}^{k} \theta_i f(a_i) \\
\text{subject to} \quad & \theta_1 \le \delta_1 \\
& \theta_i \le \delta_{i-1} + \delta_i \quad \textit{for } i = 2,\ldots,k-1 \\
& \theta_k \le \delta_{k-1} \\
& x = \sum_{i=1}^{k} \theta_i a_i \\
& \sum_{i=1}^{k} \theta_i = 1 \\
& \sum_{i=1}^{k-1} \delta_i = 1 \\
& \theta_i \ge 0 \quad \textit{for } i = 1,\ldots,k \\
& \delta_i \in \{0,1\} \quad \textit{for } i = 1,\ldots,k-1
\end{aligned}
$$

Note that the first three constraints (in combination with the fact that exactly one of the binary variables must be non-zero) ensure that θ_i is zero for all but two indices i and $i + 1$.

5. Reading and exercises

Exercise 1

A food is manufactured by refining raw oils and blending them together. The raw oils come in two categories:

Vegetable oils	Veg 1
	Veg 2
Non-vegetable oils	Oil 1
	Oil 2
	Oil 3

Each oil may be purchased for immediate delivery (January) or bought on the futures market for delivery in a subsequent month. Prices now, and in the futures market are given below (in £/ton).

	Veg 1	Veg 2	Oil 1	Oil 2	Oil 3
January	110	130	130	120	105
February	130	140	120	110	135
March	110	110	150	80	115
April	120	120	140	110	115
May	100	100	130	90	95
June	90	120	110	100	125

Vegetable oils and non-vegetable oils require different production lines for refining. In any month it is not possible to refine more than 200 tons of vegetable oils and more than 250 tons of non-vegetable oils. There is no loss of weight in the refining process and the cost of refining may be ignored.

It is possible to store up to 1000 tons of each raw oil for use later. The cost of storage for vegetable and non-vegetable oil is £5 per ton per month. The final product cannot be stored, nor can refined oils be stored. At present there are 500 tons of each type of raw oil in storage. It is required that these stocks will also exist at the end of June.

There are several technological restrictions that need to be imposed on the blending process:

(a) in the units in which hardness is measured this must lie between 3 and 6. It is assumed that hardness blends linearly and the hardness of the raw oils are:

Veg 1	8.8	Oil 1	2.0
Veg 2	6.1	Oil 2	4.2
		Oil 3	5.0

(b) if an oil is used in a month then at least 20 tons of that oil must be used.

(c) the final product cannot be made up of more than three different oils in any month unless a vegetable oil is used in the blend

(d) if a vegetable oil is included in the blend in any month then so must Oil3.

The final product sells at £150 per ton. What buying and manufacturing policy should the company pursue in order to maximize profit? How would the policy change if the range of the hardness of the final product had to be between 3 and 7?

Exercise 2

Show how each of the relationships below can be modelled with zero-one variables in either one or two constraints. (In order not to pre-judge than answer, space has been left for two constraints in every case, although in some of the cases only one constraint is required).

Where there is more than 'one' right answer, in the sense that both define the same feasible set of integer values, the required answer is the formulation which has the 'tighter' LP feasible space.

In these relationships, 'P-> Q' means 'P implies Q'; 'P or Q' means 'P or Q or both'; and 'sign' means ≤, ≥ or =.

A	B	C	D	E	sign	RHS
$-x_A$	$+x_B$				≥	0
$-x_A$	$+x_C$				≥	0

(a) A -> (B and C)

(b) A -> either B or C but not both

(c) A -> B and B -> A

(d) A -> exactly 2 of B, C, D, and E

(e) A -> not B

(f) (A and B) -> C

(g) (A or B) -> C

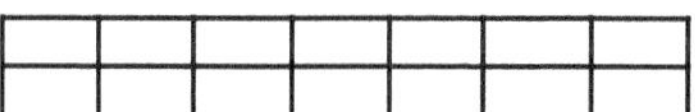

(h) no more than 3 of A, B, C, and D

(i) A -> (B or at least 1 of C and D)

(j) (A or B)-> at least 1 of C, D and E

Reading

Required: If you have some more time this week: some of the material of chapter 10 in Williams will be addressed in Lecture 15. The remainder of the chapter will be set as required reading in Lecture 15.

Recommended: Williams: chapters 9.1 to 9.4
Bertsimas/Tsitsikils: chapter 10.1

Suggested: --

OR428 – Model Building in Mathematical Programming

Lecture 13: Linear Programming VII – Network Flow Problems

Outline:
1. Graphs - some basic terminology
2. Minimum Cost Flow problems
3. Transportation Problems
4. Maximal Flow Problems
5. Shortest Path problems
6. Example
7. Reading and exercises

This lecture introduces a very important class of LP problems, which are known as *network flow problems*. These problems are important for various reasons. One reason is that they can be represented not only as a LP problem, but also as a specific mathematical object called a *graph*. Looking at problems in terms of graphs can be a helpful way of analysing them and often provides a fresh perspective on the problem. Moreover, because of their mathematical structure, network flow problems can be solved much faster than general LP problems. Therefore, from a practical perspective, the modeller is in a very convenient situation if it is possible to represent a problem as a network flow problem. Finally, network flow problems are guaranteed to have solutions that are integer if the b-vector is integer. For practical applications this can be very important, i.e. when fractional solutions do not make sense. In the following, we will have a look at the four most relevant types of network flow problems: *transportation problems*, *minimum cost flow problems*, *maximal flow problems* and *shortest path problems*.

1. Graphs - some basic terminology

All network flow problems can be represented as a graph. Here we introduce some basic terminology about graphs before we come back to the transportation problem. A *directed graph* (or else a *network*) is a set of *nodes* and *arcs* which are directed from one node to another node. In Figure 1 there are 8 vertices and 7 arcs. This example of a graph is not a connected graph as there are 3 separate components, the group {1, 2, 3, 4, 5}, group {6, 7} and an isolated node group {8}.

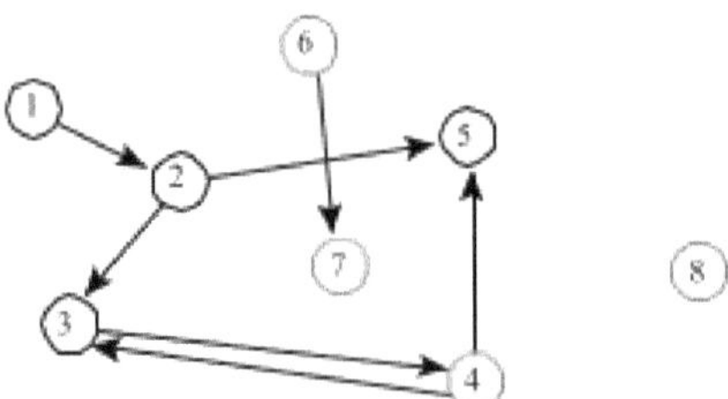

Figure 1. A directed graph with 8 vertices and 7 arcs

A way of representing a directed graph is by a *node-arc incidence* matrix. The rows of the matrix correspond to the vertices and the columns to the arcs. Cell *ij* of the matrix is -1 if node *i* is the origin node of arc *j*; Cell *ij* is +1 if node *i* is the destination node of arc *j*; otherwise cell *ij* is 0 if node *i* is not 'incident to' arc *j*. The graph in Figure 2 would be represented by the node-arc incidence matrix given in Table 1.

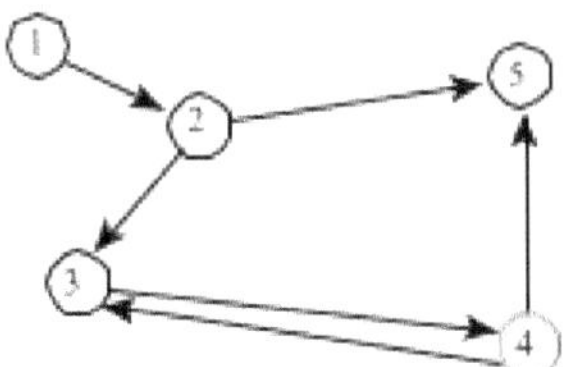

Figure 2 The directed graph for the node-arc incidence matrix in Table 1

node \ arc	1,2	2,3	2,5	3,4	4,3	4,5
1	-1					
2	+1	-1	-1			
3		+1		-1	+1	
4				+1	-1	-1
5			+1			+1

Table 1 Node-arc incidence matrix for the directed graph in Figure 2

2. Minimum Cost Flow problems

A very common problem is concerned with the distribution of a single homogeneous product from factories (*sources*) to customers (*destinations*). The amounts available at each factory and the amounts required by the customers are known. The product is sent to customers via intermediary points (warehouses or distribution centres). There are capacity limitations on some of the transportation links. The objective is to minimise the total cost of meeting customer demands. This situation corresponds to the most general network flow problem, referred to as the Minimum Cost Flow problem. Consider the graph in Figure 3 below. In this example, node 1 is the origin with a supply of 20, nodes 4 and 5 are the destinations with demands of 5 and 15, nodes 2 and 3 are transhipment nodes. Each arc has a cost, e.g. arc (1, 3) has a cost of 4 and some of the arcs have a capacity (in squares), e.g. arc (1, 3) has a capacity of 8. The objective is to find the minimum cost pattern of flows that satisfies the demands.

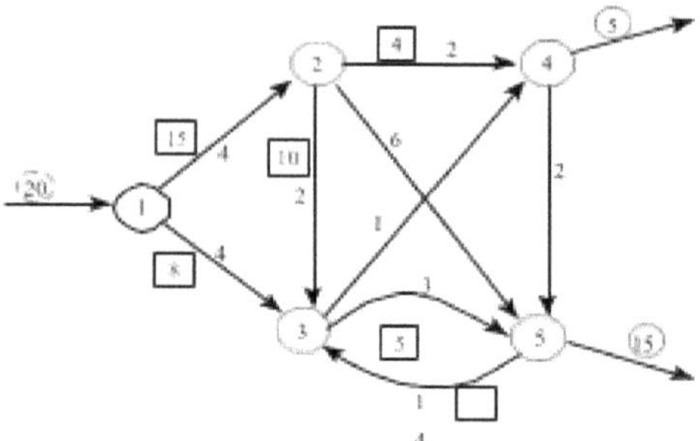

Figure 3 An example Minimum Cost Flow problem graph

The LP problem associated with the above example is given in tabular form in Table **Cost Flow problem of Figure 3**

In the above, the number of variables is the number of arcs; the number of constraints is the number of nodes. Each variable has 2 non-zero elements in its column, one +1 and one -1. The constraint matrix is the node-arc incidence matrix of the network; the non-zero elements in the column of the arc (i, j) are -1 in the row node i and +1 in the row node j.

3. Transportation problems

There are known quantities of a homogeneous commodity available at m sources in set S, and known quantities required at n destinations in set D. The cost of transport from each source to each destination is known, and the problem is to find that pattern of distribution from sources to destinations which will minimise transport cost. Let the costs of transporting a unit of commodity between source i and destination j be c_{ij} for $i = 1, 2, ..., m; j = 1, 2, ..., n$. The availability at the sources is a_i for $i = 1, 2, ..., m$ and the demand at the destinations is b_j for $j = 1, 2, ..., n$. The total demand is not more than the total supply, that is: $\sum_{i=1}^{m} a_i \geq \sum_{j=1}^{n} b_j$. The non-negative variable x_{ij} is the amount to be transported from source i to destination j. The problem can be formulated as a linear programme (notice that this is a special case of a Minimum Cost Flow problem with no intermediate nodes):

$$\min \sum_{(i,j)\in A} c_{ij} x_{ij}$$

s.t.

$$-\sum_{\{j:(i,j)\in A\}} x_{ij} \geq -a_i \quad \forall i \in S$$

$$\sum_{\{i:(i,j)\in A\}} x_{ij} \geq b_j \quad \forall j \in D$$

$$l_{ij} \leq x_{ij} \leq u_{ij} \quad \forall (i,j) \in A$$

4. Maximal Flow problems

In this problem we wish to send as much flow as possible from a specified source node, s, to a specified destination node, t, the sink. There are no costs on the arcs of the network but there are capacities. The general formulation is as follows (note that we maximise an artificial flow from the sink to the source, an arc that we may have to add to the graph if it does not exist):

$$\max \quad x_{ts}$$

s.t.

$$\sum_{\{k:(k,i)\in A\}} x_{ki} - \sum_{\{j:(i,j)\in A\}} x_{ij} = 0 \qquad \forall i \in N$$

$$l_{ij} \le x_{ij} \le u_{ij} \qquad \forall (i,j) \in A$$

In the example in Figure 4 below we wish to find the maximum flow from source node 1 to sink node 6. The values associated with the solid arcs are the capacities. The dashed arc is introduced to the graph to model this as a Maximal Flow problem.

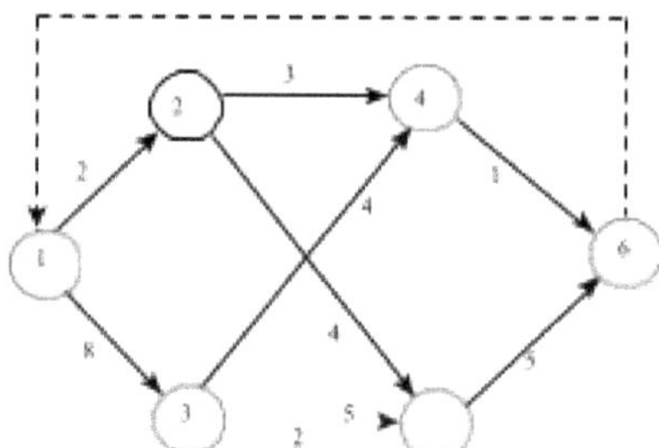

Figure 4 An example graph of a Maximal Flow problem

5. Shortest Path problems

The shortest path problem is a particular network flow model that has received a lot of attention for both practical and theoretical reasons. The problem can be stated as follows: Given a network with cost c_{ij} associated with each arc (i, j), find the cheapest path through the network from a specified source to a specified sink (destination). The theoretical interest in the problem arises because it has a special structure, in addition to being a network, that results in very efficient solution procedures.

Representing this problem as a network flow problem is straightforward. The problem is to send one unit of flow from the source to the sink at minimum cost (distance). Let x_{ij} be the flow from node i to node j, then the formulation is as follows:

$$\min \quad \sum_{(i,j)\in A} c_{ij} x_{ij}$$

$$s.t. \quad \sum_{\{k:(k,i)\in A\}} x_{ki} - \sum_{\{j:(i,j)\in A\}} x_{ij} = \begin{cases} -1 & if\ i = s \\ 0 & otherwise \\ 1 & if\ i = t \end{cases}$$

$$x_{ij} \geq 0 \qquad \forall (i, j) \in A$$

6. Example: Scheduling Production and Inventory

Consider a factory producing a particular product, the demand for which varies over time. There are three methods of adjusting the volume of output to meet the fluctuating demand:

- *(i) regular production up to a limit of r units per month at a cost of £a per unit;*
- *(ii) overtime production up to a limit of v units per month at a cost of £b per unit;*
- *(iii) store the product from one month to the next at a cost of £c per unit per month.*

The factory's planning horizon is 3 months and the demand is d_1, d_2, and d_3 units in each month respectively.

The cost of meeting demand at minimum total cost can be formulated as a minimum cost flow problem. The nodes M1, M2, and M3 are the three months, RT1, RT2, and RT3 are regular time in the three months, and OT1, OT2, and OT3 overtime. Figure 5 below illustrates the network structure. To write the Minimum Cost Flow formulation, let reg_t, $over_t$ and $store_t$ be the non-negative variables. Then the formulation is:

$$\min a\sum_t reg_t + b\sum_t over_t + c\sum_t store_t$$

$$\begin{aligned} s.t. \quad & reg_1 + over_1 - store_1 \geq d_1 \\ & reg_2 + over_2 + store_1 - store_2 \geq d_2 \\ & reg_3 + over_3 + store_2 \geq d_3 \\ & 0 \leq reg_t \leq r,\ 0 \leq over_t \leq v,\ store_t \geq 0. \end{aligned}$$

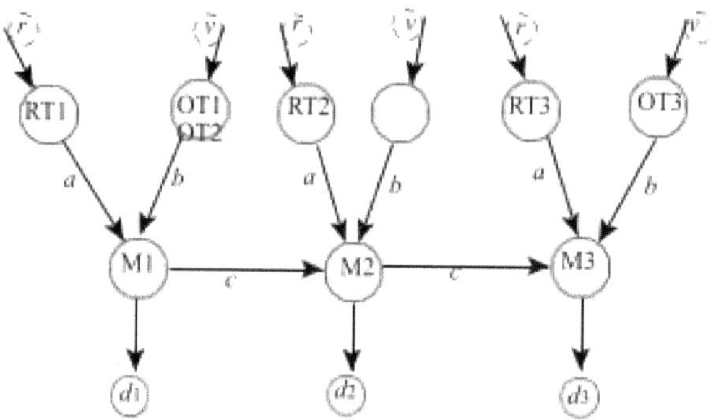

Figure 5 Graph of the production and inventory example

7. Reading and exercises

Reading:

Required: chapters 5.3 and 5.4 in Williams (1999).

Recommended: Go through chapters 3 and 5 of Williams (1999). Most of the more important material has been covered in the previous lectures, but you will find many interesting details, in particular some remarks on objective functions that are possible with Linear Programming in chapter 3.2, the "modal formulation" of a model at the end of in chapter 3.4, the "Assignment Problem" and the "Critical Path Analysis" as two more network applications of Linear Programming in parts of chapter 5.3, and some remarks on converting Linear Programming problems in network problems in chapter 5.4.

Suggested:

(1) chapters 8 and 9 of Hillier / Liebermann (2001). [The material of this lecture is covered in chapters 8.1, 9.1 - 9.3, 9.5 - 9.6 of Hillier/Liebermann. Assignment and all types of network flow problems are covered in detail in OR408.]

(2) have a look at the book Network Flows by Ahuja *et al* (1993) to get an idea of the large number of applications of network flow problems

Exercises:

Exercise 1

A firm producing fashion goods at two plants close to Shanghai and Guangzhou, respectively, each with a maximum capacity of 1100 cases (collections) per week, has a contract to make regular weekly deliveries of 500 cases to New York, 400 to Berlin, 1000 to London, and 300 to Paris. Cost of transport by sea (in £s per case):

	Guangzhou	London	Paris	New York	Berlin	Rotterdam
Shanghai	1.00	3.00	2.70			
Guangzhou		2.50		5.00		2.00
London				4.00		
Rotterdam				2.80	1.00	

(a) Model the problem, represent it with AMPLDev in the form of separate model and data files, and find the minimum cost pattern of transport, using these facilities only.

(b) China Southern has entered the Skyteam alliance, and as a result air-freight rates have been reduced. A sales manager draws the headquarter's attention to the fact that the four weeks average delivery period (regardless of choice of route) to New York and the two and a half weeks to Europe is costing the firm money in the capital tied up in the 'pipeline'. The goods are worth £1000 per case, the rate of interest on capital is 0.2% per week, and air-freight rates from Guangzhou to New York and Rotterdam (including carbon off-setting) are £15.00 and £10.00 per case, respectively. Should the firm use air-freight, and, if so, how should it re-arrange its deliveries? (Assume that air-freight and all European routes take zero time, while the sea transport from Rotterdam to New York takes one and a half weeks.)

Exercise 2

Single-duty crew scheduling: The following table illustrates a number of possible duties for the drivers of a bus company. We wish to ensure, at the lowest possible cost, that at least one driver is on duty for each hour of the planning period (9 am to 5pm). Formulate and solve this scheduling problem as a shortest path problem.

Duty hours	9-1	9-11	11-2	12-3	12-5	2-5	1-4	4-5
Cost	30	18	35	21	38	20	22	9

Exercise 3

A company has two factories, one at Liverpool and one at Brighton. In addition it has four depots with storage facilities at Newcastle, Birmingham, London and Exeter. The company sells its products to six customers C1, C2, ..., C6 (see the diagram below). Customers can be supplied from either a depot or from the factory direct.

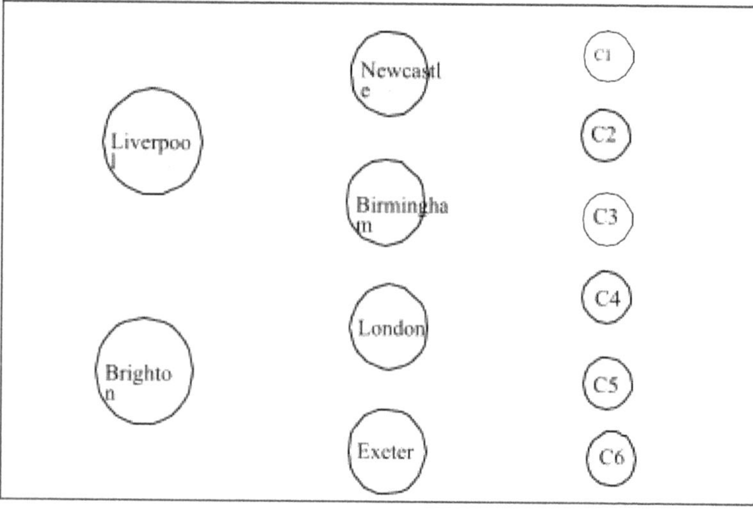

The distribution costs, in £ per tonne delivered, are known; they are in given below where a dash indicates that a supplier cannot supply a particular customer or depot.

Supplied to	Supplier					
	Liverpoo l factory	Brighton factory	Newcastl e depot	Birmingham depot	London depot	Exeter depot
Depots						
Newcastle	0.5	-				
Birmingham	0.5	0.3				
London	1.0	0.5				
Exeter	0.2	0.2				
Customers						
C1	1.0	2.0	-	1.0	-	-
C2	-	-	1.5	0.5	1.5	-
C3	1.5	-	0.5	0.5	1.5	-
C4	2.0	-	1.5	1.0	-	1.5
C5	-	-	-	0.5	0.5	0.5

C6	1.0	-	1.0	-	1.5	1.5

Each factory has a monthly capacity given below which cannot be exceeded:
Liverpool 150,000 tonnes
Brighton 200,000 tonnes.

Each depot has a maximum monthly throughput given below which cannot be exceeded:
Newcastle 70,000 tonnes
Birmingham 50,000 tonnes
London 100,000 tonnes
Exeter 40,000 tonnes

Each customer has a monthly requirement below which must be met: C1 50,000 tonnes
C2 10,000 tonnes
C3 40,000 tonnes
C4 35,000 tonnes
C5 60,000 tonnes
C6 20,000 tonnes

The company would like to determine:

i. What distribution pattern would minimise total cost?

ii. What would be the effect of increasing factory and depot capacities on distribution costs?

iii. Certain customers have expressed preferences for being supplied from factories or depots to which they are accustomed. The preferred suppliers are:

C1 Liverpool (factory), C2 Newcastle (depot),
C5 Birmingham (depot), C6 Exeter or London (depots)

Is it possible to meet all customers' preferences regarding suppliers and if so what is the extra cost of doing so?

OR428 – Model Building in Mathematical Programming

Lecture 14: Modelling Environments IV – Using AMPL Script

Outline:

1. Introduction

After having used AMPLDev in a very simple way since Lecture 1, we have learned, from Lecture 6 on, to represent more complex Linear Programming problems with the programming language AMPL by writing separate model and data files. In terms of Lecture 5, this means that we have learned to represent the *declarative knowledge* of a model with AMPL.

What we have not done yet is to represent the *algorithmic knowledge* of a model. Until now this has not been necessary because the matrix-generator, the pre-solver, the solver and the report generator that work within the AMPLDev environment contain so much (implicit) algorithmic knowledge that we could fully rely on it for solving problems. However, for more complex problems it is helpful to go beyond the standard algorithmic knowledge that is incorporated in AMPLDev.

The means of representing specific algorithmic knowledge in AMPL is an *AMPL script file*. This lecture is meant to give you an introductory overview of what AMPL script files can do. Moreover, we will address the most important case of using an AMPL script, which is the import and export of data from files outside the AMPL environment (from an Excel file, for example). Finally, this lecture presents a slightly more advanced example, which shows that AMPL script files can also include commands that are typically part of general-purpose programming languages. It illustrates that script files such as AMPL scripts provide us with very flexible means of using the methods of Mathematical Programming to design algorithms that are tailored to the needs of very specific optimisation problems.

2. The different functions of a script

The general function of a script consist in controlling (and, if necessary, modifying) the entire process of representing a model by means of a computer. This involves all stages from making available the model structure (or several model structures) and the model data, controlling the pre-solver and the solver, and preparing and analysing the output data. The following diagram illustrates this.

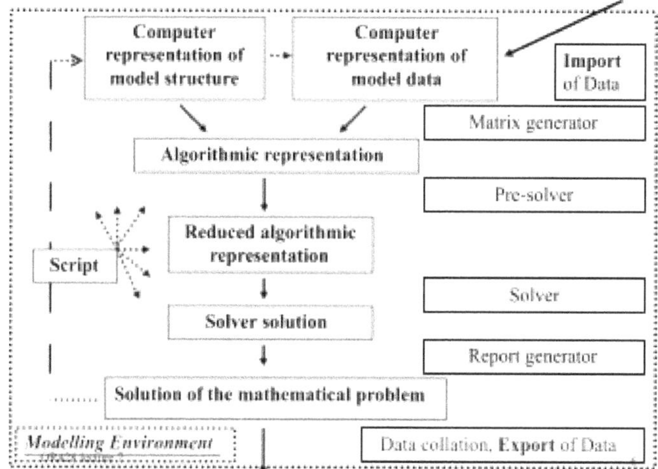

Depending on the problem that the modeller intends to solve, a script file might also be used for organising the process of solving several (similar or different) sub-models and exchanging data among them. In this way, rather complex models with a large number of variables can often be solved in a reasonable amount of time.

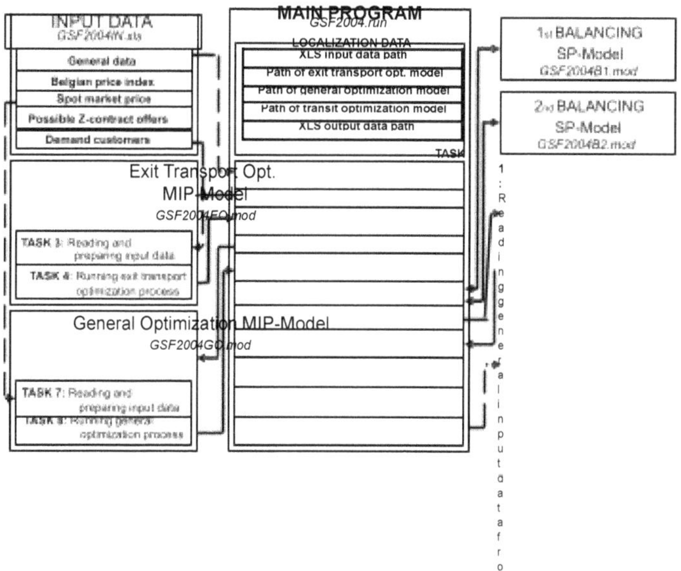

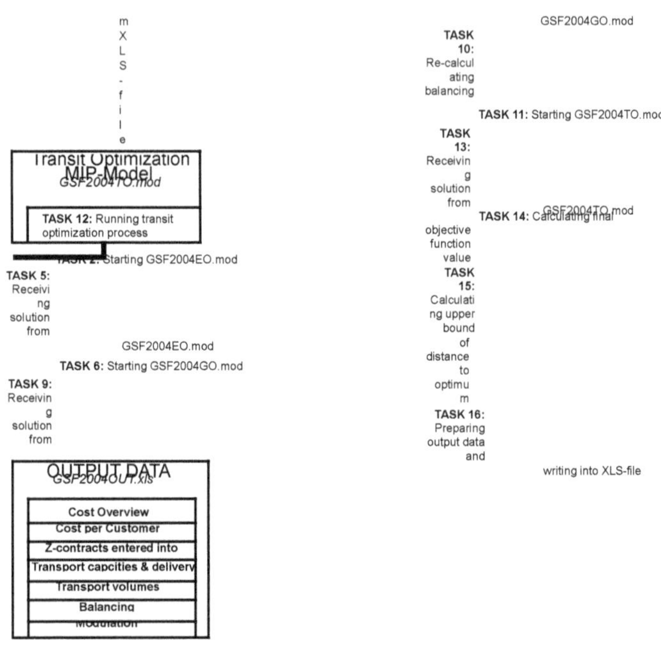

Example of a complex optimisation model controlled by a script

The diagram above illustrates a case in which a script file, the 'MAIN PROGRAM', reads data from an Excel file 'GSF2004IN.xlsx', coordinates 5 Mathematical Programming models ('GSF2004EO.mod', 'GSF2004GO.mod', 'GSF2004B1.mod', 'GSF2004B2.mod', and 'GSF2004TO.mod') and finally writes the result into another Excel file, which is called 'GSF2004OUT.xlsx'.

Related to the process illustrated in the first diagram above, we can distinguish between the following main functions of a script:

1. To define a particular (sub-)model, i.e. a model file and, if necessary, a data file.
2. To import/export data from/to outside the modelling environment.
3. To calculate parameters for a particular (sub-) model on the basis of given data.
4. To modify a particular (sub-)model, i.e. a model file or a data file.
5. To determine the way in which a (sub-)model is (pre-)solved and initiate the process of (pre-)solving it.
6. To calculate certain quantities related to the solution of a (sub-)model.
7. To display parameters, the solution of a (sub-)model, or related quantities on the screen or write them to a file or a printer.

In order to fulfil these seven functions, scripts are written in a programming language that is not only designed specifically for these functions, but also includes the standard concepts that can be found in all-purpose programming languages (such as C++, Visual Basic, JAVA, Pascal, etc.). Typically, these standard concepts include definitions, conditional expressions, loops, conditional loops, functions, etc. This implies that a modeller using a script is flexible to go for any combination of solution methods that lies between the 'extreme points' of the default setting of AMPLDev (including a standard solver setting) and an entirely customised, newly-created algorithm for the problem at hand.

It is important to be aware of a fundamental difference between script files on the one hand and model and data files on the other.
Representing the declarative knowledge of a mathematical model, model and data files contain expressions that *define* or *describe* a problem. When writing a model or a data file, we use expressions like 'set', 'param', 'var', 'minimize' or 'subject to' in order to define parameters, variables, the objective function or the constraints. What we do not do is to tell the computer how to solve the mathematical model, i.e. what to do about these parameters, variables, constraints, etc. Model and data files are solely about describing or declaring a model.
In contrast to this, script files represent algorithmic knowledge for solving a problem. This means that they mainly contain *commands*, that is expressions that tell the computer what to do. Often, some preliminary definitions are necessary for doing this, but these are not the main components of a script file; the algorithmic knowledge of a model as represented in a script file is about giving orders to the computer.

3. Import and export of data with AMPL scripts

Many practical applications require a large amount of input data from different sources and a detailed analysis of the solution of a model. As a consequence, the use of data files (.dat files) is clearly limited. Therefore importing data from an Excel file (or a database) and exporting data to them is one of the most important areas of application of script files. In the following, we will demonstrate the basic concepts of data import and export by drawing on the probably most famous classic LP problem, the *Diet Problem*. As the most common source of data in practical applications is an Excel file, we will focus on this. The import and export of data with a database is not much different from this. (See AMPLDev User Manual, AMPL Studio User Manual and/or the book on AMPL by Fourer et al. for details.)

3.1 The Diet Problem and its AMPL model file

The Diet Problem consist in determining the amounts of different types of food to be bought such that the food bought contains at least a certain minimal amount of nutrients and does not contain more than a certain maximal amount of nutrients, and the amount of money spent on buying the food is minimal. (This problem has also practical industrial relevance because it has the same structure as the problem of determining the optimal mix of products during a production process.)
The model looks as follows:

Index sets: F — set of types of food

I — set of nutrients contained in the food

Parameters:

n_i^{min} — minimal amount of nutrient i that the food must contain, $i \in I$

n_i^{max} — maximal amount of nutrient i that the food must contain, $i \in I$

$a_{i,f}$ — amount of nutrient i that one unit of food of type f contains, $i \in I$, $f \in F$

c_f — cost of one unit of food $f \in F$

Variables: x_f — amount of food of type f to be bought, $f \in F$

Objective: minimise $\sum_{f \in F} c_f * x_f$

Constraints:

$\sum_{f \in F} a_{i,f} * x_f \geq n_i^{min}$ for all $i \in I$

$\sum_{f \in F} a_{i,f} * x_f \leq n_i^{max}$ for all $i \in I$

$x_f \geq 0$ for all $f \in F$

A suitable AMPL model file for this problem is:

```
# MODEL FILE Lec12DietProblem.mod

### SETS #######################

set NUTR;          # Types of nutrient
set FOOD;          # Types of food

### PARAMETERS #############

param cost {FOOD};        # Cost per unit of food param n_min
{NUTR}; # Lower bound on nutrients param n_max {NUTR};    #
Upper bound on nutrients param amount {NUTR, FOOD};
#Nutrients per unit of food

### VARIABLES ################
var BuyV {FOOD} >= 0;              #Units of food to be bought

### OBJECTIVE FUNCTION #####

minimize Total_Cost:
      sum {f in FOOD} cost [f] * BuyV [f]; ###

CONSTRAINTS ############

subject to

DietMin {i in NUTR}:
     sum {f in FOOD} amount [i, f] * BuyV [f]
>= n_min[i];

DietMax {i in NUTR}:
      sum {f in FOOD} amount [i, f] * BuyV [f]
<= n_max[i];
```

3.2 Writing AMPL script files as a part of an AMPL project

If we prefer to use an Excel file that contains the sets and parameters (instead of an AMPL .dat file), we have to write an AMPL script file. For using an AMPL script file, you have to proceed as follows:

1. have an existing AMPL project with a model file (and maybe an additional data file) ready,
2. if you have a 'script' folder, right-click and create a new file (->New -> script file), otherwise you can create a new file in .txt, rename it to *.run and drag it into the script folder

3. write your script into the new window that opens,
4. execute your script (change 'Run Configuration' to run the script file only, and untick 'Solve after executing the files listed above').

3.3 How to import and export data with an AMPL script

We have to proceed in six steps, the first of which is about making the necessary preparations in Excel, the next two of which provide AMPLDev with the necessary *definitions* and the last three of which are *commands* that tell AMPLDev what to do:

1. Prepare the tables in Excel.
2. Tell AMPLDev the model file that the data is used for.
3. Tell AMPLDev the details about the Excel tables that you would like to read and to write into.
4. Tell AMPLDev to read the model data from the tables.
5. Tell AMPLDev to solve the model.
6. Tell AMPLDev to write the solution into the tables.

Step 1: Prepare the tables in Excel

The data that we would like to import consists of the index sets and the vector parameters. Each of the parameters corresponds to a sub-table in Excel with the first column (or the first columns) containing the indices that the parameter in question depends on. These 'index columns' are called the key columns of a sub-table. They are important for two reasons: a) we will use them to import the index sets, and b) as they contain the indices of the vector parameter, they will help AMPL as a means of organising the rest of the data in a sub-table.

For every parameter, we have to perform the following tasks (unless we build a sub-table that contains several parameters):

First we have to define within Excel a range, i.e. the sub-table that is meant to contain the data of the parameter. For doing so, select via the top menu: Insert -> Name -> Define... and then choose a name and define the range for the sub-table (in newer Excel version: Formulas -> Define Name -> Define Name). The name can be chosen arbitrarily but it is helpful if it is related to the name of a related AMPL model entity.

Second we have to prepare the sub-table in Excel by giving a headline to all columns. The first column(s) of a table are KEY COLUMNS that contain the combinations of indices to which the parameter values in the columns which follow correspond. For example, in the case of the parameter $a_{i,f}$, we require the first two columns of a table in Excel to be the key columns and contain all combinations of the names of nutrients i and food f, while a third column contains the amounts of nutrient i per unit of food f. So for a table that contains the values of the parameter $a_{i,f}$, the first row would contain the names of the columns, e.g. "FOOD", "NUTR", "amount" (using the same names in the Excel file as in the AMPL file is convenient but not necessary – see e.g. the figure below and the discussion of the next steps), while the second to the last row contain the values of the indices and the parameter, with the values of the indices of the parameter given in the first two columns and the value of the parameter given in the third column.

After having done this for all parameters, we prepare similar tables for the output data. If convenient, we do not have to set up completely new sub-tables for parameters that are defined over the same domain or for solution values which are to be written to the Excel file by AMPL following the solution of the model, but we can add, where appropriate, some more columns to sub-tables that already exist. The screenshot in Figure 1 illustrates the structure of the data in the Excel file for the diet problem presented earlier.

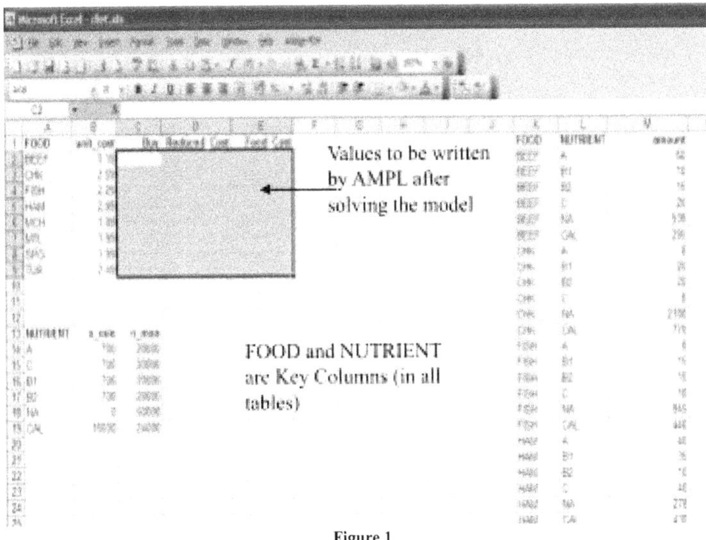

Figure 1

Step 2: Define the model files in AMPL

In order to let AMPLDev know which model we would like to solve later and which model structure is the one that AMPL has to combine with the data, we use the word 'model', followed by the name of the file that contains the model structure. (Note that, if the model file is not in the same folder as the script file, the name of the model file has to include the name of the path of folders where the file can be found.) So, if our model file is called "diet_script", we write:

```
model diet_script.mod;
```

The easier way to tell AMPLDev which model file to run is via Run Configurations. You add the model file, followed by the script file and untick "Solve after executing the files listed above".

Step 3: Define in AMPL the sub-tables you would like to read and to write into

This step is the most detailed one as we have to give AMPL all information about the structure of the specific sub-tables that we created in Excel and inform AMPL about the way in which we would like to use the tables (i.e. which index set, parameter, or solution value corresponds to which part of the Excel tables).
The most basic structure of a definition of a sub-table in AMPL is as follows:

- the word "table",
- an (arbitrary) name that we give to this sub-table in AMPL,
- the word "IN" for a table that is used for reading data, the word "OUT" for a table that is used for writing data, and no word at all for a table that is used for both reading and writing data,
- the word "ODBC" (in double quotation marks!), which is short for "Open Database Connection" and informs AMPL that it is about to use a Microsoft standard-protocol for reading and writing data,
- the name and path of the Excel file that contains our data (in double quotation marks!),
- the name of the sub-table in Excel (in double quotation marks!), i.e. the name of the range in question, as defined in Step 1 above,
- a colon,
- a list of the key-columns of the sub-table in Excel, separated by commas and written into square brackets "[ ]", another comma,
- a list of the other columns of the sub-table in Excel, again separated by commas, and
- a semi-colon at the end.

<u>Example</u>:

```
table dietNutrs IN "ODBC" "diet.xlsx" "Nutrition":
     [NUTR],
     n_min
     ,
     n_max
     ;
```

This AMPL script definition is about the parameters 'n_min{NUTR}' and 'n_max{NUTR}' in the Diet Problem model file. It explains to AMPL that

- there is a table that we will refer to as "dietNutrs" within the script file, that
- is used for reading data only ('IN'),
- uses the Open Database Connection protocol to read from the Excel file 'diet.xlsx' (located in the same directory as the AMPL model), specifically from a sub-table (range of cells) in that file that has been named 'Nutrition'
- consists of the key column 'NUTR' (which will contain the elements of the index set 'NUTR' in our AMPL model file), and
- contains two more columns, namely 'n_min' and 'n_max', from which we will read the values of the parameters 'n_min' and 'n_max' (defined in the AMPL model file).

Now that we have had a look at the basic principles of defining a table with AMPL script, we will address some more details about the lists of key-columns and other columns in the following, which will allow for a more professional use of the table-related features of AMPL script.

1. Normally, i.e. by default setting, key-columns are not used for reading data; only the other columns after the key-columns are used in this way. If we would like to <u>read</u>

the values of a key-column into AMPL (in this case the element of the set 'NUTR'), we have to write:

```
NUTR <- [NUTR]
```

(instead of just `[NUTR]`)

The former formulation tells AMPL script that we would like to read the key-column '[NUTR]' and that its values shall populate the set 'NUTR'. (This implies that we can give different names to the AMPL set and the Excel key-column. The statement

```
NUTR <- [NUTRIENT],
```

for example, would explain to AMPL that we are interested in reading a key-column called 'NUTRIENT' and use its values as members of an AMPL set called 'NUTR'.

2. If we would like to import the values of a vector parameter with two indices, we write, as indicated above, both parameters in square brackets, separated by commas. For example, the expression:

```
table dietAmounts IN "ODBC" "diet.xlsx" "Amounts":
    [FOOD, NUTRIENT],
    amount;
```

is used to define a table for the parameter 'amount{FOOD, NUTR}'. Note that the name of the second key column ('NUTRIENT') is different from the name of the corresponding set in AMPL ('NUTR'), however this is fine as AMPL "knows" that the parameter 'amount' is defined over the domain {FOOD, NUTR} so it will know that the two key columns (whatever their names might be) will just populate the domain for this parameter.

3. If we were to import data for a scalar parameter, say a scalar parameter called 'nmax', we would not need a key-column and therefore write

```
table dietAmts IN "ODBC" "diet.xlsx" "Amounts":
    [],
    nmax;
```

4. We have seen above that the key-column in Excel and the corresponding index set in AMPL can have different names. This is also possible for the other columns. If the columns in the Excel table and our parameters in AMPL have different names, we have to write, for example,

```
table dietAmts IN "ODBC" "diet.xlsx" "Amounts":
    [FOOD, NUTR],
    amount ~ amnt;
```

in order to let AMPL know that the values of the AMPL parameter 'amount' are to be read from an Excel column called 'amnt'.

5. All these syntactical rules apply also to writing data into tables. As mentioned above, we just have to use the word 'OUT' in the definition of the table instead of the word 'IN'. If, for example, we would like to define a table into which we can write the solution of the model (the values of the variables 'BuyV' in our case) and their reduced cost, we just have to write

```
table Solution OUT "ODBC" "diet.xlsx" "Solution":
    [FOOD],
    BuyV,
```

```
BuyV.rc;
```

which tells AMPL that we have a sub-table, called 'Solution' both within the script and within Excel, with the key-column [FOOD] (in Excel), in which we would like to write the values of the variables BuyV and their reduced cost.
(On this occasion: if you would like to write the dual values of some constraints into a table remember that in AMPL the dual values of a constraint are referred to by writing the name of the constraint concerned. So similarly to writing 'BuyV' in the statement above to refer to the primal variables, we could to write 'DietMin' to refer to the dual values of those resource constraints that make sure that the diet calculated contains at least a certain minimum amount of the nutrients – because 'DietMin' is the name of these constraints in the AMPL model file above.)

6. When we write data into a table, we can even calculate new values. The statement

```
table Solution OUT "ODBC" "diet.xlsx" "Solution":
    [FOOD],
    BuyV,
    BuyV.rc
    ,
    {j in FOOD} cost[j] * BuyV[j] ~ Food_Cost;
```

for example, amends the previous table by a fourth column, which contains for every type of food the amount of money that we will have to spend on it (cost[j] * BuyV[j]); the statement "…~ FoodCost" tells AMPL that this column is called "Food_Cost" in Excel.

7. As mentioned above, it is also possible to use the same table for both reading and writing data, which might be convenient in some cases. In such a case, we do without the words 'IN' or 'OUT' at the beginning of the table definition, and, instead, write at the end of the statements that describe the individual columns whether a certain column is used for input or output purposes. This could lead to a definition like the following (which contains some more of the features mentioned above):

```
table dietFoods "ODBC" "diet.xlsx" "Foods":
    FOOD <- [FOOD] IN,
    cost ~ unit_cost IN, BuyV
    ~ Buy OUT,
    BuyV.rc ~ Reduced_Cost OUT,
    {j in FOOD} cost[j] * BuyV[j] ~ Food_Cost OUT;
```

Once we have finished our definitions of the different tables within AMPL script, it is time to move to the next step.

Step 4: Tell AMPL to read the model data from the tables you have defined

So far we have just *defined* the tables in AMPL and told it how they should look like with an external data source, i.e. an Excel file. What we need now is *commands* to actually read the tables and assign the data to values of parameters within AMPL. Fortunately, this step is much more straight forward: we only need to write the commands 'read table' and the name of the table in AMPL, followed by a semi-colon. The command

```
read table dietAmounts;
```

for example, written in conjunction with the definition in 2. above, reads the values of the parameter amount{FOOD, NUTR} from a column called 'amount' in an Excel sub-table called 'Amounts'.
Similarly, the command

```
read table dietFoods;
```

(in conjunction with the definition in 7. above), reads the elements of the AMPL set 'FOOD' from a key-column called 'FOOD' and the values of the parameter 'cost{FOOD}' from a column with the name 'unit_cost' (the other columns in this definition refer to output data and are therefore not affected by this command).

Step 5: Tell AMPL to solve the model

Once we have imported all the necessary data from the Excel sub-tables into AMPL, we can tell AMPL to solve the model. For doing so, we write the command

```
solve;
```

As we have told AMPL in Step 2 which model file we are talking about, we do not need to provide any further information.

Step 6: Tell AMPL to write the solution into the tables you have defined

This step works similar to Step 4. In this case, the command is 'write table', i.e. the command

```
write table dietFoods;
```

(in conjunction with the definition in 7. of Step 3) tells AMPL to write the values of the variables 'BuyV', the reduced cost of these variables, and the values of the expression 'cost[j] * BuyV[j]' into an Excel sub-table called 'Foods'.

3.4 The AMPL script file of the Diet Problem

Using the guidelines described above we may write the following AMPL script file:

```
# SCRIPT FILE script1.run

# Define the model to be solved
# (Do this in Run Configurations) #model
 diet_script.mod;

##### TABLE DEFINITIONS################

# Define table from which data on types of nutrient
# and their minimal and maximal values are to be read later

 table dietNutrients IN "ODBC" "diet.xlsx" "Nutrition":
    NUTR <- [NUTRIENT],
n_min,
    n_max
    ;

# Define table from which data on the amounts of #
 nutrient per unit of food are to be read later
```

```
table dietAmounts IN "ODBC" "diet.xlsx" "Amounts":
    [FOOD, NUTRIENT],
    amount;

# Define table from which types of food and their cost #
are to be read and into which the solution is to be #
written later

table dietFoods "ODBC" "diet.xlsx" "Foods":
    FOOD <- [FOOD] IN,
    cost ~ unit_cost IN, BuyV
    ~ Buy OUT,
    BuyV.rc ~ Reduced_Cost OUT,
    {j in FOOD} cost[j] * BuyV[j] ~ Food_Cost OUT;

########## READ DATA #########################
# Read types of nutrient and their minimum and maximum #
values from table
read table dietNutrients;

# Read amounts of nutrient per unit of food from table

read table dietAmounts;

# Read types of food, cost of food from table read
table dietFoods;

######## SOLVE PROBLEM #####################
solve;
# display optimal solution and objective value
display Total_Cost;
display BuyV;


########## WRITE DATA ##########################

# Write the solution in the Excel file write

table dietFoods;
```

4. Example: sensitivity analysis with AMPL scripts

In the following, we will briefly sketch another example of using AMPL scripts. We assume that we have the model file for the Diet Problem and that we have a data file that contains the elements of the index sets and the parameters. What we would like to do now is to write an AMPL script that solves several instances of the model, which are characterised by different minimal values for one nutrient (vitamin 'B2' in this case). This means we are interested in the solutions that we get if we solve the problem for different values of the right-hand side of the constraint DietMin.

We need some more AMPL script commands for doing so:

- The command 'data' to tell the script where to get the data of the model from. This command works in exactly the same way as the command "model" described above.
- The command 'let', which can be used to assign values to a parameter. Here we will use it to define the values of the RHS of the DietMin constraint for which we would like to calculate the solution of the model.
- The command 'for', which repeats a certain procedure presented in '{ ... }' several times, once for each element of a given set. Here we use this to repeat the process of solving the model for every value of the RHS that we are interested in.
- The command 'display', which allows us to print the solutions of the different models we have solved on the screen. (Of course we could also export it to an Excel file by using the method described in the previous section of this lecture.)

Using these commands, we may write the following AMPL script:

```
# SCRIPT FILE script2.run
######## SENSITIVITY ANALYSIS #####################
# This script explores the impact of changing the #
 values of the parameter n_min['B2']

# load the model via the run configuration
 #model diet2.mod;

# load the data file (we assume here that the data has # been
 written into a .dat file, but we could have also # combined
 this scipt with the above one
# which reads/writes data from/into an Excel file) #
 load the data file via the run configuration #data
 diet2.dat;

# define a parameter to indicate the
# number of scenarios to be considered #
 and initialise it
param S integer; let
 S:=9;

# Define a set to contain labels for #
 the scenarios considered
set Scenarios:= 0..5;

# define a 'stepsize' for changes in values of #
 parameter n_min['B2'] inbetween scenarios and
```

```
# initialise it
param stepsize integer;
 let stepsize:=50;

#Define a parameter to contain the values of
# n_min['B2'] in each scenario and initialise it
 param ScenarioValues {Scenarios};
 let {s in Scenarios} ScenarioValues[s]:=
  n_min['B2'] - s*stepsize;

# Define Parameters to store the required results #
 for each scenario
param Cost {Scenarios}; param
 DualValues {Scenarios};

# FOR - LOOP: actions for each scenario# for
 {s in Scenarios}
 {
let n_min['B2']:= ScenarioValues[s];
      solve;
let Cost[s]:=Total_Cost;
let DualValues[s]:=DietMin['B2'];
 }

# Display commands display
 ScenarioValues; display
 Cost;
display DualValues;
```

Running this script file produces the following output on the screen in AMPLDev:

```
FortMP 3.2j: LP OPTIMAL SOLUTION, Objective = 90.0041958
FortMP 3.2j: LP OPTIMAL SOLUTION, Objective = 83.8769166
FortMP 3.2j: LP OPTIMAL SOLUTION, Objective = 77.87366944
FortMP 3.2j: LP OPTIMAL SOLUTION, Objective = 71.87042228
FortMP 3.2j: LP OPTIMAL SOLUTION, Objective = 68.60565837
FortMP 3.2j: LP OPTIMAL SOLUTION, Objective = 68.60565837
FortMP 3.2j: LP OPTIMAL SOLUTION, Objective = 68.60565837
FortMP 3.2j: LP OPTIMAL SOLUTION, Objective = 68.60565837
FortMP 3.2j: LP OPTIMAL SOLUTION, Objective = 68.60565837
FortMP 3.2j: LP OPTIMAL SOLUTION, Objective = 68.60565837
ScenarioValues [*] :=
0 700
1 650
2 600
3 550
4 500
5 450
6 400
7 350
8 300
```

```
9 250
;
Cost [*] :=
0   90.0042
1   83.8769
2   77.8737
3   71.8704
4   68.6057
5   68.6057
6   68.6057
7   68.6057
8   68.6057
9   68.6057
;

DualValues [*] :=
0 0.138413
1   0.120065
2   0.120065
3   0.120065
4   0
5   0
6   0
7   0
8   0
9   0
;
```

The sensitivity analysis presented here is just one more example of what you can do with AMPL script files. AMPL script has many more commands and these can be used in a very flexible way. You could use AMPL script, for example, for automatically determining if a model has multiple optima. For doing so, you would write a script file that first checks whether the necessary condition for multiple optima (see Lecture 8) holds. If yes, your script would set up a new model that checks if also the sufficient condition mentioned in Lecture 8 holds. As mentioned in section 2 of this lecture, scripts can also be used for combining several smaller models to solve a larger problem, or to calculate values that are helpful for analysing the solution, or changing model files, for example. In the end, the way in which AMPL script is used depends on the creativity of the modeller and the individual practical problem at hand.

5 . Reading and exercises

Exercise 1

Solve Exercise 1 of Lecture 11 using an AMPL script file that reads the model data from a suitable Excel file that you have created. Write the resulting production plan into the same Excel file. Include in your output tables the reduced cost of the variables that indicate the amount to be produced and the dual values of the resource constraints that determine the upper bound on the number of units of the different products that can be sold on the market (marketing restriction).

Reading:

Required:
Go through chapters 7 and 8 of the AMPL Studio User Manual. You do not have to work through the chapters in detail (nor to understand every bit of them). Rather you should get a general overview of various types of problems that can be addressed with a script file.

Recommended:
If you feel that you would benefit from doing more modelling exercises, have a look at part II of Williams (1999).

Suggested:
In case you have not already done so, have a look at "AMPL : a modeling language for mathematical programming" by Robert Fourer, David M. Gay, and Brian W. Kernighan (2003), who are the creators of AMPL, and read chapters that you are interested in. In chapters 10 to 14 you will find many more details of what is possible with AMPL scripts. (Library: Course Collection QA402.5 F77.)

OR428 – Model Building in Mathematical Programming

Lecture 15: Integer Programming III – Modelling Techniques II

Outline:

This lecture continues the topic of IP modelling techniques from Lecture 12. While the focus of that lecture was mainly on modelling discrete phenomena as IP problems, this lecture focuses on modelling continuous problems as IP problems. In particular, this means the following: we have seen at the beginning of this course that LP problems come with a linear objective function and a convex feasible region. In this lecture we will see that even problems without these properties can be solved by the IP approach. Apart from this, the present lecture addresses what distinguishes good from bad IP formulations. Finally, we will make a remark on the interpretation of dual values in Integer Programming.

1. More about modelling non-linear objective functions

At the end of lecture 12 we have seen that binary variables can be used to model piecewise linear objective functions. This sub-section is intended to provide more details on what characterises problems that can (or cannot) be approached in such a way.

1.1 Convex Programming

The technique that allows for modelling piecewise linear functions is much more important than it might appear at first sight. The reason for this is that in principle we can approximate every function by a piecewise linear function, i.e. by straight line segments. In order to increase the accuracy of the solution, we just have to use as many breakpoints a_1, a_2, a_3, ... , a_k as we need. In practical applications, it makes sense to increase the number of breakpoints especially in areas where we expect the solution. Often, it is helpful to calculate the breakpoints (or their distance if they are equidistant in some interval) on the basis of an upper bound that we impose on the possible error produced by the approximation. For doing so, setting up a new optimisation problem can be advisable.

A particularly favourable situation is given when we have a minimisation problem and the objective function is *convex*. We know from a previous lecture that a *set* is called convex if all points on the line between two (arbitrary) points from the set are also members of the set. A *function* is called convex if the set of all points on the graph of the function and above the graph is convex, i.e. if

$$\{(x, y) : y \geq f(x)\}$$

is a convex set. A function the negative of which is convex, i.e. $-f$ is convex, is called *concave*.

Minimising a convex function over a convex set (or maximising a concave function over a convex set) is called *Convex Programming.*

The favourable situation that is given with a convex objective function consists in the fact that we do not need the binary variables y_i when we approximate the function by a piecewise linear function with the approach used at the end of the previous lecture.

Recall that we needed the variables y_i to ensure that at most two adjacent θ_i are non-zero, while all other θ_i had to be zero. However, when we have a convex piecewise linear function (and this is the case when we approximate a convex function by a piecewise linear function), every point the co-ordinates of which are expressed by a sum of more than two non-zero θ_i, has an objective function value that is higher than the objective function value that we would get by expressing the same point as a sum of at most two non-zero θ_i. Therefore, if we have a minimisation problem, the model itself ensures that we will never have more than two non-zero θ_i – simply because the minimisation problem will always choose the alternative with the lower objective function value.

As a consequence, optimising a convex objective function is considerably faster than a non-convex one because we do not lose time by executing the Branch-&-Bound algorithm. This also implies that we can afford using much more breakpoints (and hence will have a much more precise approximation) when the objective function is convex.

As minimising a function is equivalent to maximising the negative of the function, the same favourable property is given when we maximise a concave function. In all other cases (which include cases where the objective function is neither concave nor convex), however, we have to resort to binary variables y_i in the fashion presented at the end of the previous lecture.

Notice, however, that we can decompose a function into convex and concave segments. This implies that, for each convex region, we need only one indicator variable that indicates when the values of the other variables represented in the objective function are within the convex region (independent of the number of breakpoints we use in that region). In contrast to this, the number of binary variables that we have to use in the concave regions depends on the number of breakpoints that we wish to have there. Depending on the problem at hand, such a way of decomposing the objective function into parts over convex regions (with one indicator variable each) and concave regions (with more indicator variables) can save a large amount of computational time in cases where not the entire objective function is convex. Finally, notice that for optimising convex functions special Convex Programming algorithms have been developed. These can be helpful when approximating the objective function by a convex piecewise linear function is too complicated or needs too many breakpoints for achieving the accuracy necessary for the problem.

1.2 Separable Programming

Approximating an objective function by a piecewise linear function requires one property of the underlying function that we have not mentioned yet: the function must be *separable*. A function in several variables is called separable if it can be expressed as a sum of functions in single variables, i.e. a function $f(x_1, x_2, \ldots, x_n)$ is said to be

separable if

$$f(x_1, x_2, \ldots, x_n) = \sum_{i=1} f_i(x_i) .$$

Solving an optimisation problem by means of a separable function is called *Separable Programming*.

If this condition is given, we can model each component of the sum independently as a piecewise linear function (or approximate it by a piecewise linear function).

If this condition is not given, we can, perhaps surprisingly, often transform a function into a separable function. Consider, for example, the function

$$f(x_1, x_2) = x_1 x_2 ,$$

which is clearly not a separable function. However, by introducing the variables u_1 and u_2 with

$$u_1 = \frac{1}{2}(x_1 + x_2) \quad \text{and} \quad u_2 = \frac{1}{2}(x_1 - x_2) \qquad (*)$$

we can write the product $f(x_1, x_2) = x_1 x_2$ as $u_1^2 - u_2^2$ because of

$$u_1^2 - u_2^2 = \frac{1}{4}(x_1^2 + 2x_1 x_2 + x_2^2) - \frac{1}{4}(x_1^2 - 2x_1 x_2 + x_2^2) = \frac{x_1 x_2}{2} + \frac{x_1 x_2}{2} .$$

Hence we can add the constraints (*) to the model, write $u_1^2 - u_2^2$ wherever the product $x_1 x_2$ occurs in the model, and finally approximate u_1^2 and u_2^2 by piecewise linear functions.

Another approach for arriving at a separable function that can then be approximated by a piecewise linear function consists in replacing the product $x_1 x_2$ by a variable y, adding the constraint

$$\log y = \log x_1 + \log x_2 ,$$

and approximating the logarithm by a piecewise linear function. The feasibility of this method, however, depends very much on the numerical stability of the solver the modeller uses.

Remarks:

1. The two methods presented above can be used to successively transform any polynomial function into a separable function. As any (sufficiently smooth) function can be approximated by a polynomial function, Separable Programming is a helpful approach to many problems.

2. The general concept of transforming a function into a separable one can also be applied to a constraint with a non-linear left-hand side, which allows for modelling

more complex feasible regions than the feasible regions in LPs, which are bounded by hyperplanes. The approximation of such a separable function, of course, will be (piecewise) linear again.

3. Sometimes it is – for computational reasons – not possible to use binary variables for approximating a non-convex separable objective function by a piecewise linear function. In this case, specific algorithms for Separable Programming can be used. They are a modification of the Simplex Algorithm, which makes sure that at any extreme point under consideration no more than two θ_i are basic variables. While this procedure ensures a precise evaluation of the piecewise linear function used for approximation, it cannot guarantee anymore that a 'true' global optimum is reached. In these cases, the modeller can only expect to find a local optimum.

4. Instead of transforming a function into a separable one, alternative options are possible. In particular, any function can be approximated on a multi-dimensional 'grid' for each point of which the value of the function is calculated. For all other points that are not on the grid, the value of the function is linearly approximated by the points on the grid that are in the neighbourhood of these points. (For details, see Williams (1999) at the end of chapter 9.3.) This method, however, comes with many binary variables and is therefore only rarely the method of choice.

2. Disjunctive constraints

In some applications we do not require all constraints to be satisfied simultaneously. Instead, just a certain subset of them must hold. Imagine a situation in which a company would like to make a strategic investment decision, for example, such as setting up plants in the UK, in Germany, or in both countries. Due to different markets in Germany and the UK, certain constraints might be given that model the British market, while others model the German market. Obviously, the subset of feasible points that refers to UK-only investments does not have to satisfy the constraints that model the German market, and vice versa. In other words: not all constraints of the model have to be satisfied at the same time – only a subset of them is relevant for certain decisions.

To model this situation, let us assume that we have three sub-sets $C_i := \{C_{i,1}, C_{i,2}, \ldots, C_{i,n}\}$ with $i = 1, 2, 3$ that consist of n_1, n_2, and n_3 constraints, respectively (of course, this concept can be generalised to more than 3 sub-sets of constraints). We would like to model the situation

EITHER C_1 OR C_2 OR C_3.

Such a statement is called a *disjunction of constraints*.

For modelling it, we introduce 3 indicator variables $\delta_1, \delta_2, \delta_3 \in \{0,1\}$, which are meant to indicate whether the constraints C_1, C_2, and C_3, respectively, hold. Then we simply express the relationships

$C_{i,2}$ *AND* ... *AND*

$C_{i,n}$ for $i = 1, 2, 3$

by means of the technique for indicator variables of valid constraints that we presented in sub-section 1.2 of Lecture 14, and add the constraint

$$\delta_1 + \delta_2 + \delta_3 = 1.$$

This concept can be generalised. By using the same technique, we could model the situation "at most two of the three sub-sets of the constraints must be satisfied", for example, and add the constraint

$$\delta_1 + \delta_2 + \delta_3 \leq 2 .$$

An important specific case of using disjunctions of constraints is the case where we would like to model a non-convex feasible region. In such a case, we decompose the feasible region into convex sub-sets each of which we model by a set of resource constraints. Finally, we add the indicator variables and constraints that are necessary for modelling the disjunction of these sets of constraints in order to represent the entire feasible region in our model (see Williams (1999), chapter 9.4, for a detailed example).

As a consequence, we can – at least in principle – model also non-linear feasible regions by using the Linear / Integer Programming approach. We just have to approximate the feasible region by linear constraints and apply the technique for disjunctive constraints if the feasible region is not convex. For rather complex problems, however, it might be difficult to find such an approximation, or such an approximation requires too many binary variables to be sufficiently exact, and as a result finding the optimum might require a long time.

For such cases, specific non-linear optimisation techniques have been developed. Nevertheless, the (comparably) simple and at first sight very restrictive structure of Linear / Integer Programming is surprisingly flexible, and approximations based on it often require considerably less time than other approaches (which is mainly due to the nice properties of the feasible region and the corresponding efficiency of the Simplex Algorithm and other LP methods).

3. Good IP formulations and the convex hull of the feasible region

We have seen in Lecture 13 that solving IP problems requires much more computational effort than solving LP problems. Therefore, when setting up an IP model, the modeller should reflect on the question of whether the formulations chosen is computationally favourable. Obviously, the formulation of a model is computationally favourable when only a few LP problems have to be solved to find an optimal solution of the IP problem.

In order to see when only a few LP have to be solved, recall the circumstances under which Branch-&Bound fathoms a branch of the search tree:

(1) when the sub-problem is infeasible,
(2) when the sub-problem has an integer solution, or
(3) when the solution of the sub-problem has a lower objective function value (in the case maximisation) than some integer solution that has previously been found.

While improving the search of the optimal solution with respect to the last one of these criteria is primarily a matter of a smart search strategy (i.e. of the *algorithmic knowledge* that we provide), we can improve the computational time that Branch&Bound needs with respect to the first two criteria by taking care of the *declarative knowledge* incorporated in our model. That is we can try to use smart inequalities for our model.

The first one of the three criteria above suggests that we build our model such that the feasible region is as small as possible. The second criterion suggests that as many extreme points of the feasible region as possible should be integer.

This idea gives rise to the following definition:

Definition: (Convex hull of an IP)
For a given IP, the convex hull of the IP is the smallest possible convex set
that contains all feasible solutions.

Consider the following diagramme that shows the convex hull of the IP (dark grey) and the feasible region of the LP relaxation (union of light grey and dark grey sets) of the IP problem

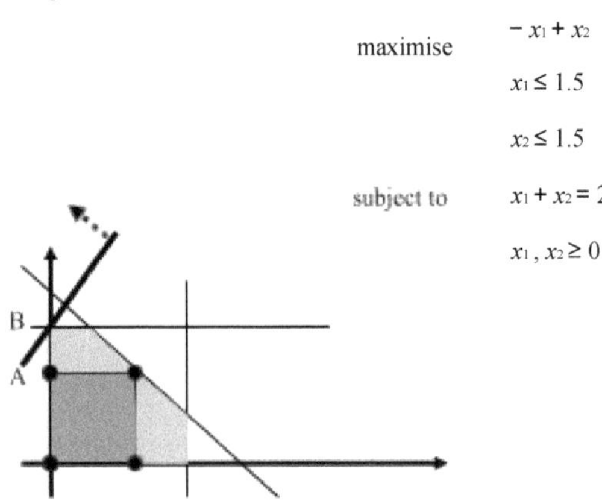

$$\text{maximise} \quad -x_1 + x_2$$

$$\text{subject to} \quad x_1 \leq 1.5$$

$$x_2 \leq 1.5$$

$$x_1 + x_2 = 2$$

$$x_1, x_2 \geq 0$$

Obviously, the IP is maximised at point A, while the optimum of the LP relaxation is point B. This means that Branch-&-Bound will need to solve at least two LP problems. If, however, we had modelled the problem by using the constraints $x_1 \leq 1$, $x_2 \leq 1$ and $x_1, x_2 \geq 0$, i.e. if we had modelled the convex hull of the problem, solving one LP problem would be enough for solving our IP problem because the optimum of the LP relaxation (point A) would also be the optimum of the IP. Such a formulation of a model is called *sharp*.

This holds in general: whenever we can model the convex hull of an IP problem (i.e. find a sharp formulation), we can be sure that solving the LP relaxation of the IP problem will provide us with the optimal solution of the IP problem.

Unfortunately, the convex hull is known for only very few subclasses of integer programming problems. In the general case, we have to resort to Branch-&-Bound or other computationally expensive approaches. However, it is always helpful to try to find a formulation that leads to an LP relaxation with a rather small feasible region. The closer we can approach the perfect formulation, i.e. the convex hull, by the way in which we set up our inequalities, the better our formulation will be. And this is likely to reduce considerably the computational time we will need to solve the problem. This is illustrated by the following examples:

Example 1

Consider a situation where a binary variable δ_A can only take the value 1 if both binary variables δ_B and δ_C take the value 1. F1 and F2 below are two valid formulations for this situation:

$$\text{F1: } \begin{cases} \delta_A \leq \delta_B \\ \delta_A \leq \delta_C \end{cases} \quad \text{and} \quad \text{F2: } 2\delta_A \leq \delta_B + \delta_C$$

If we restrict our attention to 0-1 values for the three variables, both formulations are equivalent: both exclude solutions where δ_A=1 and at lease one of δ_B and δ_C is equal to zero. This however is not true for the LP relaxations of these two formulations. To see this consider the non-integral solution δ_A=0.5, δ_B=0, δ_C=1. Since this solution is non-integral, it is beneficial that it is a-priori excluded from consideration during the Branch and Bound search. Clearly this solution violates the system in F1, but is a valid solution for F2. In general, note that the single inequality in F2 can be obtained by adding the two inequalities in F1, so it is implied by the inequalities in F1. Therefore, any solution that satisfies F1 will also satisfy F2. The converse, however is not true as we have just seen. As a result, F1 is a stronger formulation for this situation.

In general, if a binary variable θ is only allowed to assume the value 1 if n binary variables $\delta_1, \ldots, \delta_n$ all take the value 1, the formulation

$$\theta \leq \delta \ \forall i = 1,\ldots, n$$

is to be preferred to the formulation

$$n\theta \leq \sum_{i=1}^{n} \delta_i$$

Example 2

Similarly to the previous example, in the situation n binary variables $\delta_1, \ldots, \delta_n$ are only allowed to assume the value 1 if a binary variable θ takes the value 1, the formulation

$$\theta \geq \delta \ \forall i = 1,\ldots, n$$

is to be preferred to the formulation

$$n\theta \geq \sum_{i=1}^{n} \delta_i$$

One (rather easy) way of trying to find the convex hull of an IP problem is to try to convert the problem into a network flow problem. Due to a very powerful property of the A-matrix of a network flow problem called *total unimodularity* (more about this in

Williams (1999), chapter 10.2), every IP problem given by an arc-vertex incidence matrix has an LP relaxation the feasible region of which is the convex hull of the IP problem. Therefore, it is sometimes worth the effort to achieve a network flow formulation of a problem, even though such a formulation might not be obvious at first sight. In the general case, however, sharp IP formulations (or at least better IP formulations in the sense that they come as close to the convex hull as possible) are difficult to achieve and a subject of a lot of on-going research.

4. Dual values in Integer Programming

In Integer Programming the dual values produced by the solver do in general *not* have a meaning. The optimal solution of the IP will have been found as the optimal solution of a particular LP problem. However, this LP will consist of the original constraints and some other constraints that have been added during the branching process to partition the feasible region. The dual values of this LP do not give any sensitivity information. The optimal solution and the 'next best solution' may be far apart on the Branch-&-Bound tree on quite different branches. At one of the solutions there is no information about the existence or the properties of the others.

Notice, however, that some theoretical effort has been put into defining and analysing dual problems of IP problems (as opposed to the duals of LP problems that we have discussed in previous lectures and that the paragraph above refers to). Typically, these IP duals are used for deriving good upper bounds for maximisation problems (or lower bound for minimisation problems) by means of a weak duality property. Hence they provide us with an alternative approach to solving IP problems, which can also be used in combination with Branch-&-Bound. These IP duals (such as the so-called 'Lagrangean dual') must not be confused with the duals of LP problems that AMPLDev tells us.

5. Reading and exercises:

Exercises:

Exercise 1
Piecewise linear approximation:

Model and solve the following Mathematical Programme with AMPLDev (no separate data file needed) by approximating it with a piecewise linear function with 5 equidistant breakpoints.

minimise	$2x^2 + 12.5y$
subject to	$x \geq 2$
	$x + y \geq 12$
	$x \leq 4$
	$x, y \geq 0$

Exercise 2
Obnoxious Facility Location Problem

Consider the problem of locating an undesirable facility within a given (2-dimensional) polyhedral region in which there are n population centres called *points*. As the facility is undesirable, it makes sense to locate it as far away as possible from all the existing points. The obvious criterion in this case is to locate the facility in such a way as to maximize the distance from its nearest point, i.e. we are interested in *maximizing* the *minimum* of all distances of the facility to all points. This so-called 'maximin' version of the facility location problem has been considered extensively from a theoretical and a practical viewpoint. We will assume that the distance from each point has an equal weight in the objective function, i.e. that every population centre is treated equally.

Let

- F := $\{(X,Y): 0 \leq X, Y \leq 10\}$ the polyhedral region in which the facility can be located,
- (x_i, y_i) the co-ordinates of the n points with $i = 1, 2, \ldots, n$, and
- (X, Y) the co-ordinates of the facility to be located (i.e. the variables in which we are interested).

If $|X - x_i|$ and $|Y - y_i|$ denote the absolute values of the distances of a point's x- and y-co-ordinates to the facility, the problem can be stated as follows:

maximize D		
subject to	D □	$\lvert X$ □ $x_i \rvert$ □ $\lvert Y$ □ $y_i \rvert$ for all $i = 1, 2, \ldots, n$
	(X, Y) □ F,	D □ 0

This problem statement is neither an LP nor an IP. Formulate and solve with AMPL Studio (no separate data file needed) the Obnoxious Facility Location Problem as an IP problem for 6 points with the following co-ordinates: P1 = (1, 6); P2 = (3, 1); P3 = (4, 6); P4 = (8, 3); P5 = (9, 1); P6 = (10, 6). Make sure that the upper bounds on the binary variables you will need are such that they guarantee that the feasible region of the LP relaxation of the problem is as small as possible in order to achieve the computationally most efficient model.

Hints:

1. In order to model the absolute values of the distances, introduce constraints that express every (positive or negative) distance between a co-ordinate of a point and the corresponding co-ordinate of the facility *as the difference of two non-negative variables.* (Notice that this is always a helpful approach when you would like to include variables that can take negative values in a model. You can always 'circumvent' the non-negativity restriction of LPs/IPs by proceeding in this way. In LP/IP, a variable that can take both negative and positive values by having been split into a positive and a negative 'part' is called a *free variable*.)
2. Moreover, as we are interested in absolute values in this case, introduce binary variables and use the big-M method to make sure that out of every pair of these two non-negative variables at most one variable is non-zero. The bounds used for the big- M method should be as tight as possible.

Reading:

Required:	Williams (1999), chapter 10, which provides many ideas of how to improve the formulation of an IP problem. You may focus on chapter 10.1, but you should at least have an overview of the main ideas of chapter 10.2.
Recommended:	Williams (1999): the remainder of chapter 10 (on good IP formulations), chapter 7 (on convex and separable programming) and chapter 9.4 (on disjunctive constraints) Bertsimas/Tsitsikils (1997): chapter 10.2 (on good IP formulations)
Suggested:	You will find much more details on IP problems in the book "Integer Programming" by Wolsey. (See reading list.)

OR428 – Model Building in Mathematical Programming

Lecture 16: 'Soft' Constraints and Multiple Objectives

Outline:

1. 'Soft' constraints
2. 'Solving' problems with multiple objectives
3. Goal Programming
4. Exercises

1 'Soft' constraints

A constraint of the form $\sum_j a_j x_j \leq b$ excludes any solution in which the left-hand-side exceeds b_i. In some circumstances this may be realistic; for example, in a product mix this might be a quality stipulation which is legally binding; or it might represent the capacity of a piece of hardware which cannot be expanded. But in many circumstances this may represent a capacity limitation or availability of raw material which at a price may be increased. In these cases the constraint is unrealistic.

Constraints which cannot be violated are referred to as *hard constraints* whereas those that can be violated are called *soft constraints*. A soft constraint may be modelled by introducing a non-negative upwards-deviation variable d^+ which comes with a penalty $p^+ > 0$, and then minimising the total penalty as follows:

$$\min \quad p^+ d^+$$

$$\text{s.t.} \sum_j a_j x_j - d^+ \leq b$$

$$d^+ \geq 0.$$

Because $p^+ > 0$, the above achieves the effect of allowing the original $\leq$ constraint to be violated at a cost.

Similarly, a soft $\geq$ constraint $\sum_j a_j x_j \geq b$ may be modelled with use of a downwards-deviation variable d^- and a penalty $p^- > 0$ as follows:

$$\min \quad p^- d^-$$

$$\text{s.t.} \sum_j a_j x_j + d^- \geq b$$

$$d^{-} \geq 0.$$

Finally, we may model an equality constraint $\sum_j a_j x_j = b$ by using both upwards and downwards deviation variables and penalties as follows:

$$\min \quad p^- d^- + p^+ d^+$$

$$s.t. \sum_j a_j x_j + d^- - d^+ = b$$

$$d^- \geq 0$$

$$d^+ \geq 0.$$

If $p^- \neq p^+$ then upwards and downwards deviations are penalised differently. At the optimal solution either d^+ or d^- or both will be zero (Why? Hint: show this by contradiction).

The above demonstrate that a soft constraint is essentially a hybrid of an objective and a constraint. Note that the combining the objective functions associated with soft constraints, as above with the original LP problem objective function (if one exists) is not as simple as adding or subtracting the two functions. This raises the issue of how to handle problems where there may be more than one objective. We explore this in section 2. First however, we present an example of modelling using soft constraints.

Example 1

Consider a company that manufactures a particular product on n machines (each machine produces an end-product). Not all machines are of the latest technology, so their productivity differs. For each unit of raw material used in machine j, a_j units of the final product are produced. The total target production is T units and, ideally this should be met exactly, as there is a penalty p^u per under-produced unit and a penalty p^o per over-produced unit. The company wishes to minimise the total penalty costs.

We use x_j to denote the amount of raw material used in machine j. We also use a *free variable* w (unrestricted in sign) to denote the production deviation from the target T. Further, we use non-negative variables u and o to denote the total under-production and total over-production. The problem is now formulated as follows:

$$\min \quad p^o o + p^u u$$

$$s.t.$$

$$\sum_{j=1} a_j x_j + w = T,$$

$$w = o - u$$

,

$u \geq 0$

,

$o \geq 0$

w *free*

2 Solving problems with Multiple objectives

Many real-world problems involve pursuing more than one objective. For instance, in designing its production schedule, a company may want to reduce costs but also reduce production time. More often than not, it is not possible to optimise all objectives simultaneously for a given problem. In other words, making optimal decisions with respect to multiple objectives involves having to trade off the objectives. For instance, a charitable organisation which provides services that differentially benefit different population groups will have to trade off the total benefits provided to different populations.

The sub-specialty of Mathematical Programming that considers problems with multiple objectives is known as *Multi-Objective Programming* (MOP).
While it is beyond the scope of this course to examine MOP problems in detail, we consider here a few ways of dealing with the multiple objectives in (1):

(a) Solve problem p times by considering every objective function separately and compare the results.

(b) If the objectives can be ranked in order of importance then we solve p problems in which we consider the objectives in that order. We restrict every problem to the set of optimal solutions of the previous problem. Specifically, for r=1,…,p, the r-th problem is:

(2)

$$\max c^r x$$

$$s.t\ Ax \leq b$$

$$x \geq 0$$

$$c^1 x \geq \gamma^{1*} - \varepsilon^1$$

$$c^2 x \geq \gamma^{2*} - \varepsilon^2$$

$$\vdots$$

$$c^{r-1} x \geq \gamma^{r-1*} - \varepsilon^{r-1},$$

where γ^{r*} denotes the optimal objective function value of the r-th problem in the order and the terms ε^r are 'flexibility' terms. In other words, the r-th problem maximises the r-th objective subject to the original resource
constraints and the additional condition that at the optimal solution, the value
of each of the r-1 previous (and more important) objectives is not less than

ε^r below the previously identified optimal value γ^{r*} .Construct a composite objective by taking a 'weighted average' of t $p$objective vectors, using weights λ^r, r=1,…,p, such thatλ_r = 1:

r

max $\sum^p \lambda^r ($ ^{r}

$)$This

problem is
particularly acute if the different objectives are measured in different units. For
instance how do you combine 'Cost' and 'Quality'?

(c) Maximise the minimum possible objective over the feasible set. This problem may be converted into an LP problem by introducing an additional variable z and changing the objective as follows:

max z^2 x

The constraints ensure that z is less than or equal to each objective function. Because we are maximising, at the optimal solution the value of z will be as high a value as possible, i.e. equal to the minimum of the

c^r x terms. Ic^p $x\}$.

Note that in a directly analogous fashion we may solve a *Min-max* problem if our original objectives required minimisation.

(d) Goal Programming. We consider this approach separately in the following section.

3 Goal Programming

In Goal Programming each objective has a target level and we wish to achieve all goals as nearly as possible. Specifically, the r-th objective $c^r x^r$ is assigned a target T^r. We now treat meeting each target as a soft equality constraint, which is represented using deviation variables as follows (as discussed in Section 1):

$$\sum_{j=1}^{n} c_j^r x_j + d_r^- - d_r^+ = T_r \quad r=1,\ldots,p \qquad (4)$$

These constraints are added to the original LP problem. There are two possibilities for the objectives:

(a) Minimise the weighted sum of deviations, using weights λ^r where $\sum_r \lambda_r = 1$:

$$\min \sum_{r=1}^{p} \lambda^r (d^{r-} - d^{r+})$$

$$\text{s.t } Ax \leq b$$

$$\sum_{j=1}^{n} c_j^r x_j + d^{r-} - d^{r+} = T^r \;\forall i = 1,\ldots,p \qquad (5)$$

$$d^{r-} \geq 0 \; d^{r+} \geq 0 \; x \geq 0.$$

(b) Minimise the maximum deviation. This involves solving a Min-max problem by introducing a new variable z, changing the objective function to "min z" and adding suitable constraints to the original LP problem (in addition to the constraints in (7)):

$$\min z$$

$$s.t\ Ax \le b$$

$$\sum_{j=1} c_j^i x_j + d^{r^-} - d^{r^+} = T^r\ \forall i = 1,\dots,p$$

$$d^{r^-} \le z\ \forall i = 1,\dots,p$$

$$d^{r^+} \le z\ \forall i = 1,\dots,p\ d^{r^-} \ge 0$$

$$d^{r^+} \ge 0$$

$$z \ge 0$$

$$x \ge 0.$$

Finally, note that like the approaches described in the previous section, both Goal Programming approaches above may be inappropriate if the units of measurement for the objectives (and hence also the deviation variables) are incomparable.

Example 2
Consider the following 2-objective LP problem:

$$'\max' \{x_1, x_2\}$$

$$s.t.\ x_1 \leq 6$$

$$x_2 \leq 6$$

$$x_1 + 3x_2 \leq 20$$

$$3x_1 + x_2 \leq 20$$

$$x_1 \geq 0$$

$$x_2 \geq 0.$$

Let us start by considering the objectives separately. Solving with only the first objective provides the optimal solution x^A=(6,0), whereas solving with only the second objective provides the optimal solution x^B=(0,6) (Note that there exist multiple optima in both cases and because of this different software may provide different optimal solutions). A decision maker would now have to consider choosing between these two solutions according to their preferences.

Now let us consider a priority order for the objectives, namely that the first is more important than the second. Solving with the first objective provides the solution x^A as before. We now restrict the solution set by adding the constraint x_1=6 (with no flexibility term), i.e. we solve the following problem:

$$\max x_2$$

$$s.t.\ x_1 = 6$$

$$x_2 \leq 6$$

$$x_1 + 3x_2 \leq 20\ 3x_1 + x_2 \leq 20\ x_1 \geq 0$$

$$x_2 \geq 0.$$

This provides a new solution x^C=(6,2), which is the best solution associated with the particular priority order for the objectives. Note here that if we had specified that the second objective is more important than the first then we would have ended up choosing a different solution, namely x^D=(2,6).

Finally, let us consider composing the objectives using a weighted average. Using weights equal to 0.5 for both objectives and solving the new LP problem provides yet another solution, namely x^E=(5,5).

4 Exercises

Question: *Does using equal weights mean that the objectives are equally important? Why?*

OR428 – Model Building in Mathematical Programming

Lecture 17: Integer Programming IV – The Travelling Salesman Problem

Outline:

1. Hamiltonian paths and the Travelling Salesman Problem (TSP)
2. Examples and variants of the TSP
3. Modelling the TSP with sub-tour barring constraints
4. Modelling the TSP with commodity flow constraints
5. Reading and exercises

In the previous three lectures we have introduced the concept of Integer Programming, presented the main method for solving them and discussed some modelling techniques. This lecture introduces a particular type of Integer Programming problem, the famous Travelling Salesman Problem (TSP). This type of problem has been chosen among various special types of IP problems due to the fact that it has attracted very much research, primarily because it can be stated easily, but it is surprisingly difficult to solve for larger instances of the problem. Moreover, it has many practical applications, and finally it provides us with the opportunity to enhance our understanding of graphs and learn some new modelling techniques.

1. Hamiltonian paths and the Travelling Salesman Problem

In Lecture 11, we have considered *directed* graphs, i.e. graphs in which the nodes are connected by arcs that emanate from some node and terminates at some other node. A graph is called *undirected* if the edges of the graph do not have such a direction. Every undirected graph can be transformed into a directed graph by replacing each edge by two arcs, one into each direction.

For a given undirected graph with *n* nodes $a_1, a_2, \ldots, a_n$ and some edges, a

Hamiltonian path is, loosely speaking, a 'walk' along the edges of the graph that visits every node exactly once. More precisely speaking, it is an ordering of the nodes such that every node (except the last one) and its successor in the ordering are connected by an edge of the graph.

A *Hamiltonian cycle* (or *Hamiltonian circuit*) is a Hamiltonian path that returns to its starting node.

The following diagram of an undirected graph shows a Hamiltonian path (the bold lines) and a Hamiltonian cycle (the bold lines and the dashed line).

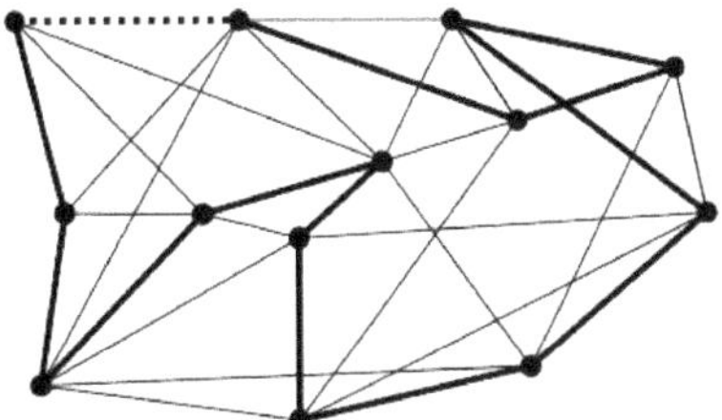

For every edge of the graph, we can introduce the 'length' of the edge (or the *cost* of walking along the edge). For a given undirected graph, the *Travelling Salesman Problem* (TSP) consists determining a Hamiltonian cycle on the graph that has the lowest cost of all possible Hamiltonian cycles. The name of the problem originates from the problem of determining the cheapest cost at which a travelling salesman can visit a number of cities once and return home. If the costs of travelling from one city to another one are dependent on the order of cities, the TSP is called *asymmetric*, if the cost of travelling from A to B equals the cost of travelling from B to A, the TSP is called *symmetric*. In the following, we will assume an asymmetric problem as this is the more general case.

Notice that the concepts of the Hamiltonian path, the Hamiltonian cycle and the TSP can analogously be introduced for directed graphs. In the following we will consider only the undirected case.

2. Examples and variants of the TSP

The TSP has many applications (and many variants, which lead to even more applications). We will just give some examples and variants:

<u>Machine drilling:</u> In the manufacture of digital equipment many holes have to be drilled in a plate. The position of the holes is known and, in the simple case, the size of the holes is identical. The drill head moves over the plate drilling the holes. Typical applications have some hundreds of holes in a plate and many plates are required on a daily basis. Moving the drill head from a hole to another takes time. The problem is to determine the sequence in which the holes are to be drilled in order to minimise the time taken to drill all holes in a plate.

<u>Minimum cost Hamiltonian path:</u> Some problems do not require the 'salesman' to return 'home', that is a minimum cost Hamiltonian path in the graph is sought. This problem can be modelled as a TSP if we set the cost of travelling 'home' from any city to zero. Alternatively, if we would like to model the problem without any pre-defined 'home' (i.e. starting point of the trip), we can add another city (a 'dummy' city) that can be reached from all cities and from where we can get to all cities, and this at costs of zero.

M Travelling Salesmen Problem: Consider that there are M possible salesman, and n cities all of which must be visited only once. All the salesmen start at some depot ('home') and return there. The objective is to schedule all salesmen to minimise total travelling cost. This problem can be modelled as a TSP by replicating the depot node M times, i.e. by having a graph M nodes of which have the same edges and distances / cost with respect to all other cities, and all M depot nodes are connected among each other with zero cost. The following diagram shows a solution of a 3 Travelling Salesmen problem with 5 cities, in which one salesman visits cities 1, 2 and 4, another one visits cities 3 and 5, and the third one does not visit a city at all (bold lines). The depot nodes are marked by D1, D2 and D3 and are connected to each other and to the same cities (thin lines and relevant bold lines). The dashed lines show some arbitrary additional connections between some of the five cities.

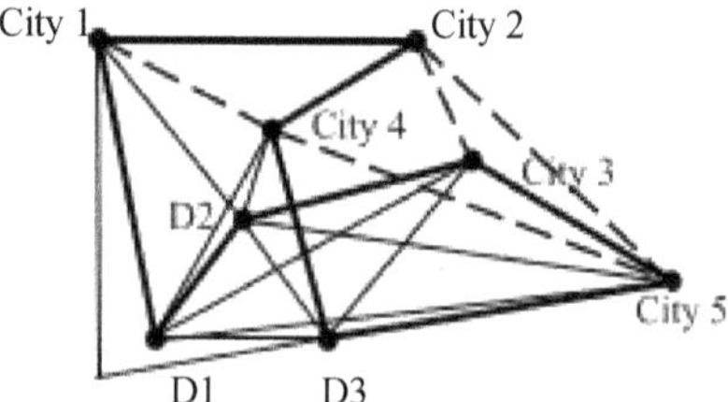

The M Travelling Salesmen Problem has important applications in calculating airline schedules (with the planes being the 'salesmen') and in vehicle routing (for distributing goods to customers from a wholesale depot by a fleet of vans, for example).

Clustered Travelling Salesman Problem: In the Clustered TSP, the set of nodes is partitioned into several sets ("clusters"). A solution to the Clustered TSP is a cycle that visits all nodes in one cluster first before moving to the next cluster of nodes. The Clustered TSP can be transformed into the standard TSP by adding an (arbitrarily) large constant M to all cost of arcs between the clusters. In this way, the model will prefer not to jump around between clusters more often than necessary, i.e. it will provide us with a solution in which the cycle visits all nodes of a cluster first before moving to the nodes of the next cluster.
Applications of the Clustered TSP can be found in warehouse planning problems, scheduling production processes, cytology and testing integrated circuits, for example. Also, Microsoft solves a Clustered TSP when minimising the defragmentation time of a hard disk (the clusters are all bits of data that belong to the same file).

Generalised Travelling Salesman Problem: Also in the Generalised TSP, the set of nodes is partitioned into clusters. Here we look for a solution with minimal cost in which we visit each cluster at least once, or, in another version of the Generalised TSP, in which we visit each cluster exactly once. By using a smart way of defining the cost (and doubling all nodes), the Generalised TSP can be transformed into a Clustered TSP, which in turn can be transformed into the 'normal' TSP (see Laporte and Palekar, 2002). Applications of the Generalised TSP include designing the material flow systems in a production plant, post-box collection, and (stochastic) vehicle routing, for example.

3. Modelling the TSP with sub-tour barring constraints

The TSP can be modelled in many ways. (Have a look at Paul William's website where you will find eight different ways of modelling the TSP and an analysis of the size of the feasible region of them.) In the following, we will introduce the classical approach to the TSP that was developed by Dantzig, Fulkerson and Johnson (1954).

The cities are represented by a set of nodes $N := \{1, 2, ..., n\}$ with c_{ij} being the cost of travelling from city i to city $j \in N$. We introduce binary variables $x_{ij} \in \{0, 1\}$, which are 1 if city j is visited immediately after city i and zero otherwise. The objective function is given by

$$\sum_{i,j \in N, i \neq j} c_{ij} x_{ij} .$$

Regarding the resource constraints, we have to make sure that every city is left exactly once:

$$\sum_{j \in N, j \neq i} x_{ij} = 1 \qquad \text{for all } i \in N,$$

and that every city is entered exactly once:

$$\sum_{i \in N, i \neq j} x_{ij} = 1 \qquad \text{for all } j \in N.$$

Until now, this problem is a special case of the transportation problem. Imagine that all cities are represented as a source node and again as a destination node. Then the above model states that every source node has an outgoing flow of exactly one, and every destination node has an incoming flow of exactly one. This particular type of transportation problem is called an *assignment problem*. (Imagine that the source nodes are people, and the destination nodes are jobs. Then the solution of the model represents an optimal assignment of people to jobs.)

Being a network flow problem, the assignment problem can be solved easily by using the LP relaxation (remember section 4 of the last lecture). However, in its present form the model is not complete because it does not make sure that the solution is *one* Hamiltonian cycle. Instead, the present model makes only sure that the solution consists of *several* cycles (called *sub-tours* in the TSP). In order to avoid these sub-tours we have to add constraints that prevent these sub-tours from being part of the solution. These constraints are called *sub-tour barring constraints*.

Imagine a sub-tour that consists of three cities 1, 2, 3. If we add the constraint

$$x_{12} + x_{21} + x_{13} + x_{31} + x_{23} + x_{32} \leq 2 ,$$

it will not be possible for the model to come up with a solution that contains a cycle

city 1 -> city 2 -> city 3 –> city 1

because this would make the left-hand side of the constraint take the value 3.

We can prevent all possible sub-tours from occurring in the solution of the model if we add constraints of the form

sum of all connections between cities in a subset $S \leq |S|$ - 1

for all possible subsets $S \subset N$. That is, we add the constraints

$$\sum_{i,j \in S} x_{ij} \leq |S| - 1 \qquad \text{for all } S \subset N .$$

These constraints are exponential in number. In practical applications, one would start without them (i.e. with the assignment problem only). When a solution with certain sub-tours has been found, we add those constraints that forbid exactly these sub-tours and solve the model again. By repeating this procedure we will finally arrive at a solution without sub-tours, which is optimal. (If we write an appropriate AMPL script file, this process of successively solving the models with additional sub-tour barring constraints can be carried automatically.)

4. Modelling the TSP with commodity flow constraints

An alternative way of modelling the TSP involves a modelling technique that is very useful for many applications. It is based on the idea that there is an (artificial) flow along the tour of the travelling salesman, and the salesman leaves one unit of the flow at every city he visits.

In addition to the assignment problem formulation, we add (continuous) variables $y_{ij} \geq 0$ that represent the flow from city i to city j. The necessary constraints to model the commodity flow concepts are as follows:

(1) Flow is only on connections that are part of the tour:

$$y_{ij} \leq (n-1)\, x_{ij} \qquad \text{for all } i, j \in N,$$

(2) $n-1$ units of the commodity flow from city 1:

$$\sum_{j \in N} y_{1j} = n-1\,,$$

(3) one unit of the commodity flow is delivered at each city, except city 1:

$$\sum_{i \in N} y_{ij} - \sum_{i \in N \setminus \{1\}} y_{ji} = 1 \qquad \text{for all } j \in N, j \neq 1.$$

5. Reading and exercises

Reading:

Required: Chapter 9.4 from Williams (1999). This text is meant to give you an overview of several other types of IP problems.

Recommended:

Suggested:

- Chapter 8.3 of Hillier/Liebermann about the assignment problem;
- Laporte et al (1996): Some Applications of the Generalised Travelling Salesman Problem, in: Journal of the Operational Research Society, 47, 1461-7;
- Laporte et al (2002): Some Applications of the Clustered Travelling Salesman Problem, in: Journal of the Operational Research Society, 53, 972-6.

Exercise:

Cardboard boxes are made from flat sheets of cardboard which is 'scored' on the fold lines. Scoring is done with scoring incisors mounted on a bar. A run of the scoring machine consists of placing the sheets of cardboard that are to become boxes flat on a table, then adjusting the incisor positions and moving the bar carrying the incisors over the boxes. There is a minimum distance α between a pair of adjacent incisors. Each box may have many fold lines to be scored, but during each run of the machine only two fold lines per box are being scored. Different types of boxes require different score lines, which are characterised by their distances from the edges of the box. From an aerial view, the score lines of a sheet of cardboard look as follows:

Two boxes may be adjacent on the table if the sum of the adjacent score distances is at least equal to the minimum distance α. So in the diagram below the pattern of sheets is feasible if

$$a_2 + b_1 \geq \alpha, \qquad b_2 + c_1 \geq \alpha, \qquad \text{and} \qquad c_2 + d_1 \geq \alpha .$$

The widths a_1 and d_2 do not matter.

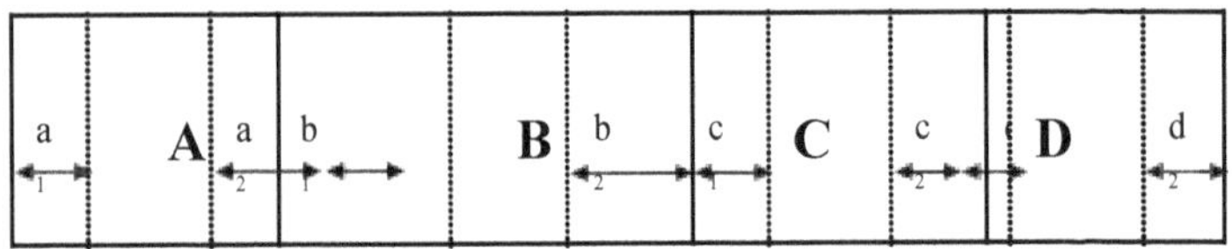

The boxes may be rotated by 180 degrees as in the diagram below (only box B has been rotated in this example, but all boxes can be rotated arbitrarily). This new pattern of sheets is feasible if

$$a_2 + b_2 \geq \alpha, \qquad b_1 + c_1 \geq \alpha, \qquad \text{and} \qquad c_2 + d_1 \geq \alpha .$$

Again, the outer widths a_1 and d_2 do not matter.

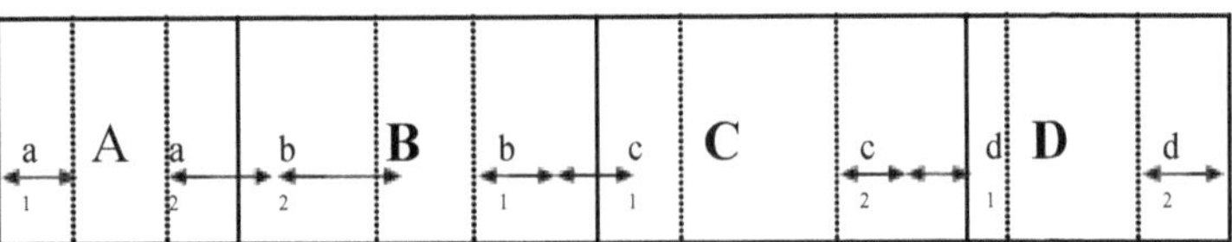

The total width of the table is T. Given n boxes of known widths and their required scoring lines the problem is to determine table-loads of feasible incisor positions so as to minimise the total number of runs of the machine.

Formulate this problem as a variant of the TSP.

Hints:

Solving this problem might be done in several steps, in any case it needs some creativity. To make it easier for you, these steps are described in the following. (Of course, you can also ignore the hints and try to find your own approach; there exist many different formulations.)

a) Step 1: Model each side of a box (the left side and the right side) as a node in a graph and set up a TSP with sub-tour barring constraints the solution of which is a feasible path of boxes with respect to the minimum distance between a pair of adjacent incisors. (The objective function does not matter here, you can set all cost to zero.)

b) Step 2 : Extend your model from step 1 to an M Travelling Salesmen Problem with M being the number of boxes. Every salesman represents a run of the scoring machine. If you define the cost function in an appropriate way, you will be able to minimise the number of salesmen (runs) you need.

c) Step 3: Extend your model from step 2 by adding the restriction that the width of the table (the maximal length of one run) is T. You can achieve this by modelling an appropriate commodity flow along the edges of the graph.

Lecture 18: Stochastic Programming I – Optimising the Expected Value

Outline:

1. Example: a strategic decision on power plants
2. Non-stochastic approaches to the power plants problem
3. The Stochastic Programming approach to the power plants problem
4. EVPI and VSS
5. Reading and exercise

All Mathematical Programming topics discussed so far assumed that all the information was known with certainty. The only exception to this was the topic of sensitivity analysis, which considers what would be the effect on the solution of changing some values. However, sensitivity analysis assumes that only one value changes at a time and leaves the user to select from a possibly large number of solutions the 'best' under some criterion. Moreover, it does not allow us to represent properly the likelihood of several changes of the model data. Models that incorporate uncertainty by drawing on probability distributions are known as stochastic models – in contrast to deterministic models, which do not.

In the following we will illustrate the basic concept of Stochastic Programming (SP) by an example in which we minimise the expected values of the cost that our decision incurs. Also, we will compare the solution of our SP model to the solutions of deterministic models and, for doing so, introduce the concepts of the expected value of perfect information (EPVI) and the value of the stochastic solution (VSS).

1. Example: a strategic decision on power plants

This example is about determining the capacity of new power plants. There are four sources of power available to generate electricity: coal, nuclear power, hydro-electricity and imported electricity.

The capital costs and operating costs for the fuel types are known. Because of the environmental impact the total capacity from coal and hydro that may be installed is limited.

The demand for electrical power is at two levels: the base load and the peak load above the base.

The base load lasts for 24 hours and the peak load is 6 hours. It is assumed that the demand is known and unchanging from day to day.

The problem is to determine which generating capacity to install and which capacity will be used to meet the demands. This problem can be formulated as a linear program.

Let p index the set *plant_types*, m index the set *operation_levels*, and let *environment* be a subset of *plant_types*, that is $environment \subset plant\_types$.

The data (parameters) of the model are:

$capital\_cost_p$	the capital cost of plant type p (£/Mw)
$operating\_cost_p$	the operating cost of plant type p (£/hr/Mw)
$duration_m$	the length of level m (hr)
$demand_m$	the demand per hour at level m (Mw/hr)
$environ\_lmt$	the environmental capacity limit (Mw).

The variables are:

$capacity_p \geq 0$	the capacity of plant type p to be installed (Mw)
$allocate_{pm} \geq 0$	capacity of plant p used at level m (Mw/hr)

The constraints are:
demand must be met at every level:

$$\sum_p allocate_{pm} \geq demand_m \; \forall m$$

the capacity allocated must be less than the capacity installed at each plant:

$$\sum_m allocate_{pm} \leq capacity_p \; \forall p$$

the environmental limit must not be exceeded:

$$\sum_{p \in environment} capacity_p \leq environment\_lmt$$

The objective function is minimise the sum of the capital costs and the operating costs:

$$\min \sum_p \left(capital\_cost_p * capacity_p\right) + \sum_p \sum_m \left(duration_m * \sum_p \left(operating\_cost_p * allocate_{pm}\right)\right)$$

A data set for this model is

plant-types are: coal, hydro, nuclear, import
levels: base, peak
capital_cost (£/Mw): coal: 200, hydro: 500, nuclear: 300, import: 0
operating-cost (£/hr/Mw): coal: 30, hydro: 10, nuclear: 20, import: 200
duration (hr): base: 24, peak: 6
demand (Mw/hr): base: 8.25, peak: 2.5
environ_lmt (Mw): 11.

Solving this model gives the solution:
coal: 2.5Mw and hydro: 8.25Mw with a total cost of £7055.

Different demand patterns
It is known that the demand pattern will change throughout the year. Each demand pattern is called a scenario as shown in the table below:

Demand (Mw)	Scenario 1	Scenario 2	Scenario 3	Scenario 4
base	8.25	10	7.5	9
peak	2.5	2	2.5	1.5

The probability of each scenario is given as 0.25.

2. Non-stochastic approaches to the power plants problem

Wait and See
Using the model on each of the demand scenarios gives

	capacity (Mw)				
scenario/plan	coal	hydro	nuclear	import	total cost (£)
1	2.5	8.25			7055
2	2	9	1		8200
3	2.5	7.5			6500
4	1.5	9			7230

The expected cost of the plans is £7246.25. This value of the expected total cost is called the 'wait and see' expected cost, z_{WS}. It is the expected value if it were possible to wait until the demand was known and then install the capacity.

Cheapest
If plan 3 were to be implemented (2.5Mw coal and 7.5Mw hydro installed) then it would be ideal if the demand pattern was always scenario 3. However, should the demand pattern be scenarios 1, 2 or 4, then electricity would have to be imported giving the costs shown below.

scenario 1	scenario 2	scenario 3	scenario 4
7805	10250	6500	7910

Total costs of the scenarios when plan 3 is implemented:

Demand

total cost

The expected cost of the scenarios is £8116.25.

Average demand
The average demand is base: 8.6875 and peak: 2.125. Applying the model to this demand pattern gives install plant types
coal: 2.125Mw and hydro: 8.6875Mw with a total cost of £7236.25.
This cost will be referred to as z_{av}, notice that it is lower that the expected 'wait and see' cost, z_{WS} of £7246.25.

If the capacity suggested by the average demand model were installed, that is 2.125Mw coal and 8.69Mw hydro, then what would be the allocation pattern? Electricity will be imported if there is insufficient capacity.

	usage of capacity (Mw)				
scenario	coal	hydro	nuclear	import	total cost (£)
1	2.06	8.69			7146.5
2	2.12	8.69		1.19	9370.3
3	1.31	8.69			6876.5
4	1.81	8.69			7349

The expected cost of the scenarios is £7685.58. This value of the expected total cost in called the 'implemented average' expected cost, $\overline{z}_{av}$.

3. The Stochastic Programming approach to the power plants problem

Clearly we need to balance the cost of the investment decisions with the expected operating costs. This leads to a model that minimises the expected cost over all scenarios. The stochastic model can be formulated as a linear program.

Sets

Let p index the set *plant_types*, m index the set *operation_levels*, and let *environment* be a subset of *plant_types*, that is *environment* $\subset$ *plant_types* and s index the set *scenarios*.

Data

The data of the model are:

$capital\_cost_p$ the capital cost of plant type p (£/Mw)
$operating\_cost_p$ the operating cost of plant type p (£/hr/Mw)
$duration_m$ the length of level m (hr)
$demand_{ms}$ the demand per hour of level m (Mw/hr) in scenario
s $environ\_lmt$ the environmental capacity limit (Mw).
$probability_s$ the probability of scenario s

Variables

The variables are:

$capacity_p \geq 0$ the design capacity of plant type p (Mw)
$allocate_{pms} \geq 0$ capacity of plant p used in level m (Mw/hr) in scenario
s E_cost_s the expected operating cost of scenario s

Constraints

The constraints are:
demand must be met in every scenario s and level m:

$$\sum_p allocate_{pms} \geq demand_{ms} \; \forall (m, s)$$

capacity used must be less than the capacity installed at all plants under all scenarios:

$$\sum_m allocate_{pms} \leq capacity_p \; \forall (p, s)$$

the environmental limit must not be exceeded:

$$\sum_{p \in environment} capacity_p \leq environment\_lmt$$

The expected cost of scenario s is

$$E\_cost_s = \sum_m \left(duration_m * \sum_p \left(operating\_cost_p * allocate_{pms} \right) \right)$$

The objective function is

$$\min \sum_p \left(capital\_cost_p * capacity_p \right) + \sum_s probability_s * E\_cost_s$$

Solving this model gives an expected total cost of £7573.75 with the design capacities:

coal: 2Mw, hydro: 7.5Mw, nuclear: 2.5Mw

The allocations are:

	allocation				excess capacity (Mw)	Total cost (£)
	coal	hydro	nuclear	imported		
Scenario 1					1.25	7405
base		7.5	0.75			
peak	0.75		1.75			
Scenario 2					0.0	8260
base		7.5	2.5			
peak	2.0					
Scenario 3					2.0	7000
base		7.5				
peak			2.5			
Scenario 4					1.5	7630
base		7.5	1.5			
peak	0.5		1.0			

The expected cost of the stochastic model, z^*, is £7573.75.

4. EVPI and VSS

Comparison of expected costs

z_{av}	average	£7236.25
z_{WS}·	wait and see	£7246.25
z^*	stochastic model	£7573.75
z_{av}	implemented average	£7685.58

Notice that the expected costs of the solutions increase. For a model that can be represented as a linear program then

$$z_{av} \le z \le z^* \le \bar{z}_{av}.$$

We define the expected Value of Perfect Information, EVPI, as:

$EVPI:=$ as $z^* - z_{WS}$,

and the Value of the Stochastic Solution, VSS, as:

$VSS := \bar{z}_{av} - z^*$.

The EVPI provides us with an idea of the amount of money that we should be willing to pay for being able to 'foresee' the future. The VSS provides us with and idea of what the additional computational effort that the SP model requires is worth. By calculating both we can give at least (very rough) upper and lower bounds on the stochastic solution in cases where calculating that is computationally not possible.

5. Reading and exercise

Reading:

Required: ---

Recommended: Birge / Louveaux (1997), chapter 1, pages 3-11, which provides a well written introduction to Stochastic Programming. (See reading list, book available in the library.)

Suggested: Birge / Louveaux (1997), the remainder of chapter 1, which includes many more examples of different types of Stochastic Programmes, and chapter 4 about EVPI and VSS. (See reading list, book available in the library.)

Exercise: (voluntary)

Airline Yield Management

An airline is selling tickets for flights to a particular destination. It can use up to six planes each costing GBP 100,000 to hire. Each plane has 12 First Class seats, 30 Business Class seats and 76 Economy Class Seats. Up to 15% of Business Class seats can be sold at Economy Class prices ('operational upgrade'), and up to 25% of First Class seats can be used for Business Class customers.
The company is considering several pricing strategies and wishes to decide a price for each of these seats. (In reality there will be further opportunities to update these prices after some time, but we will keep the model simple here. Also, we will assume that there is no cancellation option once the tickets have been purchased.)
For each class the airline considers 3 pricing options. (The same option need not be chosen for each class.) The options are as follows (all prices in GBP):

PRICES	Option 1	Option 2	Option 3
First	4,400	3,000	2,900
Business	1,800	1,600	1,200
Economy	1,000	600	400

Demand is uncertain but will be affected by price. Forecasts have been made of these demands according to a probability distribution which divides the demand levels into three scenarios. The probabilities of the scenarios are 0.1, 0.7 and 0.2 for scenarios A, B and C, respectively. The forecast demands are as follows:

DEMAND	Price Option 1	Price Option 2	Price Option 3
First Scenario A	20	30	40
First Scenario B	30	50	58
First Scenario C	40	66	72
Business Scenario A	120	140	180
Business Scenario B	80	96	112
Business Scenario C	135	150	180
Economy Scenario A	280	300	320
Economy Scenario B	300	320	400
Economy Scenario C	360	380	450

Decide price levels, how many seats to sell in each class (depending on demand) and the number of planes to book in order to maximise expected yield. (You can model the number of seats as a continuous variable.) You should schedule to be able to meet commitments under all possible scenarios. Moreover, calculate the expected value of perfect information and the value of the stochastic solution.

OR428 – Model Building in Mathematical Programming

Lecture 19: Stochastic Programming II – Types of SP problems

Outline:

1. Types of stochastic scenarios: two-stage and multi-stage SP models
2. Types of stochastic objective functions and constraints: expectation, risk, models with probability functions
3. Types of probability distributions: discrete and continuous SP models
4. Reading and exercise

In the previous lecture, we have considered an example of a SP model, discussed its relationship with certain deterministic models and, in doing so, introduced the concepts of the EVPI and the VSS. This lecture places this example in the broader context of SP problems in general and presents an overview about the main types of SP models.

1. Types of stochastic scenarios: two-stage and multi-stage SP models

The power plant problem considered in the previous lecture has the following general structure

$$\min \; cx + \sum_{s=1,2,\ldots,S} p_s q y_s$$

$$\text{s.t} \quad Ax \geq b \quad x \geq 0$$

$$Wy_s = h_s - Tx \quad \text{for} \quad s = 1,2,\ldots,S$$

$$y_s \geq 0 \quad \text{for} \quad s = 1,2,\ldots,S$$

with the variables x being given by the variables $capacity_p$, and the constraints $Ax \geq b$ represented by the constraints that make sure that the capacities of the new power plants do not exceed the environmental limit. The variables y_s are represented by the power production we allocate to the plants once we know the demand ($allocate_{pms}$), and the constraints $Wy_s = h_s - Tx$ are given by the constraints that force the model to meet the demand and prevent it from exceeding the plants' capacities. In the objective function, the term cx corresponds to the sum of the capital cost of the plants, while the term $\sum_{s=1,2,\ldots,S} p_s qy_s$ calculates the expected value of the cost of the scenarios, with qy_s being the operating cost of scenario s and p_s its probability.

The general situation can be imagined as follows: at a first stage we make the decision about the capacities of the new plants. Once we know the (stochastic) demands, at a second stage, we 'compensate' for our first decision by introducing a *recourse* $Wy_s = h_s - Tx$ that tries to balance out our first decision in the light of the result of the random process. The matrix W is called *recourse matrix*. As W does not depend on the random process, this type of model is called a *two-stage SP with fixed recourse*.

We can write this type of problem in its most general way by introducing an (arbitrary) random variable ξ (in our example above we assumed that we have a discrete probability measure) and including the case that the coefficients of the objective function and the matrix T can also be influenced by the random process. This leads to the following general definition of a two-stage SP with fixed recourse:

$$\begin{aligned} \min \quad & cx + E_\xi [Q(x, q(\xi), T(\xi), h(\xi))] \\ \text{s.t.} \quad & Ax \geq b \\ & x \geq 0 \end{aligned} \qquad (1)$$

with

$$Q(x, q(\xi), T(\xi), h(\xi)) := \begin{aligned} \min \quad & q(\xi)\, y_\xi \\ \text{s.t.} \quad & W y_\xi = h(\xi) - T(\xi)\, x \end{aligned} \qquad (2)$$

$$y_{\xi} \geq 0 .$$

The problem given by (1) is called the *first-stage problem*, while the problem (2) is called the *second-stage* problem.

The concept of a two-stage problem can be generalised to the concept of a *multi-stage problem* in which we have another random variable after the second-stage decision has been made that requires us to make another, a third decision, another random variable and a fourth decision, etc. In other words: in multi-stage problems the random variable ξ is a stochastic process, and at every stage we have to adapt the decisions made at previous stages to a new random phenomenon. The structure of multi-stage SP problems can be represented by a decision tree, and we can model it by considering every branch of the decision tree as a new scenario s. Typically, this leads to large-scale LPs (or non-linear problems) that often require specific algorithms for solving them.

2. Types of stochastic objective functions and constraints: expectation, risk, models with probability functions

The power plant example maximised the expected value of the minimal cost for running the plants. Of course, this type of models can also be aimed at making a decision that maximises the expected return. Alternatively, decision-makers may seek a decision (an investment decision, for example) that minimises risk.

In financial applications, managers and regulators often prefer a specific risk measure called *value at risk* (VaR). It describes an upper bound on the money that will get lost with a certain probability (typically $p = 0.99$) within a specific period of time. This problem can be modelled by calculating a formula for the probability distribution of the loss, approximating this formula by a linear expression and including it in the objective function (or the constraints, if the objective function aims at maximising the expected return) .

An alternative measure of risk, which often makes more sense and has nicer mathematical properties for LP models is the *conditional value at risk* (C-VaR). It is an expected value, namely the expected loss within a certain period of time conditional on the fact that a worst case event occurs (which can be defined by a probability of, say, $p = 0.01$, which represents the 1% of events with the worst outcomes).

Researchers in the field of Finance and mathematicians have developed many more measures of risk and analysed their mathematic properties (also with respect to specific aspects of SP problems), however, the VaR remains the most popular one.

Another type of SP models used frequently are models with *probability functions*. In these problems, modellers minimise (or maximise) the probability that a certain event occurs, or use constraints that stipulate that a certain event must not occur with more than a certain probability (or must occur with a minimal probability). Such a constraint could state that the probability of a certain loss (an upper bound on the VaR, for example) may not exceed 0.01. For modelling this type of problem, it is necessary to calculate the probability distribution of the event considered.

3. Types of probability distributions: discrete and continuous SP models

The power plant model that we considered has a discrete probability measure for 4 scenarios. In practical applications, people often need to model continuous probability measures such as the normal distribution, for example.

Provided that the probability distribution is not too complex, the formula of the distribution can be approximated by a linear function and included in the objective function or the constraints. This method is very limited, however, in the case of multi-stage problems. If there are only few stages with a simple structure, it sometimes is still possible arrive at a formula for the recourse function $Q(x, q(\xi), T(\xi), h(\xi))$. However, this is not an option for more complex problems. In these cases, modellers frequently generate a sample of the scenarios in the decision tree by simulation and run a discrete model with these scenarios. This procedure is repeated several times and statistic methods are used to analyse the stability of the solution.

The case of continuous probability distribution illustrates that SP problems often require the modeller to apply various different techniques to arrive at a solution. When problems go beyond the standard case of a multi-stage SP with fixed recourse, a discrete probability distribution, the optimisation of the expected value and only few stages, modellers normally have to analyse the specific structure of the problem at hand very carefully. On this basis, they can model the problem in a 'smart' way such that the problem size is reduced and the original problem is being approximated appropriately.

For solving these SP models, some special purpose algorithms have been developed that exploit the problem structure of the SP problem to tackle the large-scale models that arise from multi-stage SP problems. One of the most 'general purpose' algorithms is called *Benders decomposition.* It has been implemented into our AMPLDev version, and the language AMPL has been extended to allow for building models that provide this algorithm with the information necessary. Another area of research consists in developing algorithms that aim at an approximation of the optimal solution.

Often, modellers aim at a 'smart' model first, then draw on standard algorithms and modify them by using a script language such as AMPL script to make sure that the specific structure of their problem can be exploited successfully. In this way, many types of problems can be solved that would take too much computational effort if they were modelled 'quick and dirty' and solved with a standard solver. In view of this, it is not surprising that the field of SP is poses some of the most complex questions for research and is currently very active in developing new methods.

4. Reading and exercise

Reading:

Required: ---

Recommended: ---

Suggested: An excellent overview of the different common types of SP models can be found in Kall/Mayer (2005). The book presents many smart modelling approaches and various special purpose algorithms (see reading list, in the library). Section IV of Birge/Louveaux (1997) gives a good introduction to methods for approximating the solution of multi-stage problems.

Exercise: (voluntary)

Williams (1999), chapter 12.24, presents a four-stage version of the Airline Yield Management problem of the previous lecture. The solution can be found in chapters 13.24 and 14.24.

www.ingramcontent.com/pod-product-compliance
Ingram Content Group UK Ltd.
Pitfield, Milton Keynes, MK11 3LW, UK
UKHW062308290726
14090UKWH00018B/954

9 798895 885642